The Apostle Paul

Man of Prayer

To Kevin & Lori

May God's Best Be Yours
Carl

Advantage™
INSPIRATIONAL

Carl L. Taylor

The Apostle Paul: Man Of Prayer by Carl L. Taylor

ISBN13: 978-1-59755-258-5

Published by: ADVANTAGE BOOKS™
www.advbookstore.com

Unless otherwise indicated, all scripture quotations are from the Holy Bible, New International Version 1978, New York International Bible Society

Library of Congress Control Number: 2011931098

Cover design by Pat Theriault

First Printing: October 2011
11 12 13 14 15 16 17 10 9 8 7 6 5 4 3 2 1
Printed in the United States of America

To Margaret, who shared my life for 44 years and encouraged me to write.

To Marlys, who has shared my life for five years and who urged me to finish what I had started.

To the Congregation of the Buffalo Covenant Church

Table of Contents

INTRODUCTION

Another book on prayer? Aren't there already enough? It seems that seldom a month goes by but that another book on prayer is advertised. I have a feeling that the reason there are so many books on prayer is that most Christians, like myself, are not at all satisfied with their prayer-life. One thing is certain, it is easier to read about prayer than it is to actually pray.

As a teenager I read two books on prayer that impacted me greatly. The first was *The Preacher and Prayer*, by E. M. Bounds; the second was *Holiness in the Prayers of St. Paul*, by W. E. McCumber. The book by Bounds impressed me with the absolute necessity of becoming a man of prayer and McCumber's book introduced me to the Apostle to the Gentiles and impressed me with Paul as a man of prayer. For years I have had in the back of my mind the possibility of writing a book on prayer in the writings of the Apostle Paul. Just before I retired my wife of 44 years passed away. Working on this book has given me a wonderful objective focus as I worked through the grieving process. So whether anyone reads the book or not, it has been for me an enriching exercise.

Every Christian is in the "School of Prayer", to use a part of the title of Andrew Murray's classic study of prayer, *With Christ in the School of Prayer.* Although I have been a pastor for many years and have done my share of praying--both publicly and privately, I always realized I was still in the school of prayer and was continuing to learn how to prayer. There is a clarification and deepening insight that comes as a result writing. I remember of reading somewhere, where the author confessed, "I do not write because I understand, I write in order that I might understand." I do not write because I have a dynamic and satisfying life of prayer, or because I have found the secret for such a life, I write because I sincerely want to be a man of God and believe that prayer is fundamental to the fulfillment of this aspiration.

I have another reason for writing. I have been a student of the Apostle

Paul's writings for many years and have studied what Biblical theologians and commentators have written to explain his theology, (there is a never ending flow of books and articles to help one get a grasp on the writings and thinking of the Apostle to the Gentiles). One of the things that has fascinated me through the years is that writers on the Apostle Paul seldom mention his prayers. While there are several studies on Paul's prayers, they are either very scholarly and often not in English, or sermons which have been preached on Paul's prayers. While these are helpful and often inspirational, I wanted to explore Paul as a man who prayed. I have thus refused to yield to the temptation to deal with any depth with the prayer reports for every good commentary on Paul's writings would do this.

The approach I have taken is very simple--some would even say simplistic. I have taken the writings ascribed to Paul as being authentic representations of his mind and heart. Since he often used a secretary it may be technically inaccurate to say they are from the pen of the Apostle. I am, of course, aware that many in the scholarly community argue that a number of the letters that bear Paul's name did not come from him. I will leave this debate to the scholars. But personally, I cannot understand how anyone else could have written the intensely personal portions of these letters.

The book is divided into four parts. Part one is a study of the man, the Apostle Paul, and what we can discover about his practice of prayer from his writings. Part two is a study of Paul's teaching about prayer. We will see that the greatest contribution which Paul makes to our understanding of prayer is the teaching regarding the Holy Spirit. Part three is a study of the greetings or salutations in his letters. I believe these are much more profound and important than is generally thought. I believe the salutations reveal Paul's genius, piety, and passion. The fourth part is the appendix which contains all the references to prayer in Paul's letters and then groups them by type and makes a short annotation about each reference. The end notes generally add material which enriches that in the body of material.

It is my hope and prayer that the reading of this book will enhance your understanding of the man who wrote one-half of the New Testament, and that you will catch something of his passion and love for God as he is revealed through Jesus Christ and the inspiration of the Holy Spirit.

Rev. Carl L. Taylor

PAUL BEGAN HIS CHRISTIAN LIFE IN PRAYER

No one can doubt the importance of prayer for the Apostle Paul, for his letters are riddled with references to his prayers for the recipients, praises, and requests for prayer.[1] Yet when one reads the literature on topics related to prayer, references to Paul's letters are conspicuous by their absence. Attention is focused on the Old Testament examples of prayer, especially that of Moses, Elijah, Elisha, and David; the Psalms, which became the song book and prayer book of Israel and the church; and the life and teachings of Jesus relating to prayer. Although the Apostle Paul wrote half of the New Testament, references to what he wrote with regards to prayer are restricted generally to Romans 8; 2 Corinthians 12 and perhaps his prayer reports in Ephesians 1 and 3. My point is that if we want to enrich our life of prayer, it would be well for us to investigate the one who, more than any other figure besides our Lord Jesus himself, has shaped how the Christian faith developed and was practiced.

Luke in his history of the early church introduces us to Paul at the stoning of Stephen, then picks up the story of Paul in the account of his conversion in Acts 9. After his vision and encounter with the living Jesus, which left him blind, the Lord appeared to Ananias telling him, "*Go to the house of Judas on Straight Street and ask for a man from Tarsus named Saul, for he is praying*" (Acts 9:11). It seems as though the great sign which impressed God was the fact that Paul was praying. In fact, the Greek literally reads "for behold ("look!" "see" -- the word almost carries a feeling of surprise and delight), he is praying!"

Now Paul had been a man for whom prayer had always been a vital aspect of his life. He tells us that he was "*a Hebrews of Hebrews; in regard to the law, a Pharisee; as for zeal, persecuting the church; as for legalistic righteousness, faultless.*" (Philippians 3:5-6). As a devout

Pharisee, Paul would have kept to the prayer discipline of praying three times a day, fasting once a week, and attending the services of prayer in the synagogue.[2] According to Richard Longnecker[3] evidence of Paul's Rabbinical and Pharisaic background can be seen in his prayers, which Longnecker argues, reflects the content and emphasis of the eighteen benedictions, which were the traditional prayers of the first century Judaism.[4] It would indeed be strange if Paul's Christian prayers did not reflect something of the worship and prayer heritage which had shaped his life and faith up to his encounter with the living Jesus. We must never forget that the Christian faith has its roots in, shares in the expressions of worship with, and is the fulfillment of Israel's religion as seen in the Old Testament and developed through the intertestamental period.

In the Acts 9 account, God seems to be impressed by the fact that Paul was praying. There is a great deal of difference between saying prayers and really praying. Saying prayers (whether written by others or free prayers) can be done with a certain detachment, a complacency of spirit, an "O humness" of one who is doing his duty. Even "O hum" prayers are better than no prayer at all, however, as the very act of praying affirms one's dependence on God. But when one becomes really involved in his/her prayer there is an intensiveness, an involvement that energizes and changes the prayer itself.

That Paul, after his encounter with the living Christ, should now be really praying is not surprising. Just think what had happened to him.

1. He has had a vision of the Lord Jesus which has totally turned his theological and belief system on its head. He knew that the vision was from heaven, (this was no pleasant day dream, or figment of his imagination! It knocked him to the ground and blinded him) and the man in the vision identified himself as "*Jesus, whom you are persecuting.*"

2. The vision meant that in his efforts to serve God and please God, he had actually been opposing God. Can you imagine what a shock that was to the Pharisee who was devoted to serving and obeying God!

3. The identification of the man in the vision as "Jesus," must have

shaken his whole belief system. There was no question that the vision was from God. Jesus did not identify himself as an angel sent from God, but as "*Jesus, whom you are persecuting.*"

Now Paul had to reflect on the heretical teaching he was trying to stamp out, that believed that Jesus was the Christ, that he suffered and died, and was raised from the dead, and that he had been exalted to God's right hand and was now THE LORD! It is significant that when Ananias came to Paul he addressed him: "*Brother Saul, the Lord--Jesus, who appeared to you on the road as you were coming here--has sent me...*" Jesus is not just the Messiah, but the Lord. This facet of the faith of the followers of Jesus was what made it heretical in the view of Paul and the Jewish religious leaders. If Jesus was THE LORD, then Paul, rather than serving God was actually in opposition to God!

For three days Paul was in the night of blindness and fasted and prayed, before Ananias came to him. One can only imagine the intensity of these conversations with God. But when Ananias came, Paul was ready and did not challenge Ananias' statement: "*Brother Saul, the Lord -- Jesus...*" He arose, was baptized and received the Holy Spirit.

So Paul's Christian life really began in prayer. Although we may be people who pray, when we enter a time of darkness and confusion and are unable to control the events of our lives, our prayers take on a whole new aspect--a seriousness, earnestness, an intensity that was not there before. It is then that we discover God in new ways. And the new discovery of God changes forever how we approach our God in prayer.

This brings us immediately into the fundamental issue of prayer -- God. Our conception of God will determine how we pray, and even if we pray. This is a topic we will touch on again and again in our study, but let me observe at this point that the experience of Jesus as the Lord changed Paul's concept of God. God could no longer be thought of as far away, the austere One, or He who is so holy as to be unapproachable. In Jesus, the Almighty God revealed in the Old Testament has come close and rather than dispensing judgment has sent his Son Jesus to take the judgment and punishment which we deserved upon himself. The fact of the man Jesus, changed Paul's understanding of God. One of the results of this change is that one of Paul's favorite designations for God is that he is "*the God and Father of our Lord Jesus Christ.*" As a Jew who daily prayed the Eighteen Benedictions, Paul worshipped the God of Israel and in the prayer even referred to him as "Father". The Damascus road experience, however, revealed to him that the God of Israel is *the God and Father of the Lord Jesus Christ,* and that Jesus is messiah, savior and Lord. This revelation changed Paul's life forever and must have served as the basis of his preaching in Damascus soon after his conversion. Later he would write: *God was reconciling the world to himself in Christ, not counting men's sins against them* (2 Corinthians 5:19).

From the moment of his encounter with Jesus, Paul lived under a new vision, not only of God but of what it meant to serve God. Rather than serving God out of a sense of doing one's duty or attempting to earn his favor, Paul now had a whole new motive for service -- gratitude. There was a new sense of wonder which characterized Paul as long as he lived. He expresses this wonder 20 years after his conversion this way in his letter to the Galatians: Jesus *"loved me and gave himself up for me*" (Gal. 2:20). And his other letters indicate that he was filled with wonder that he, a persecutor of the church, should be called to be an Apostle of the very faith he tried to destroy. The sense of gratitude even enabled him to face the suffering of deprivation and prison with the amazing joy of being accounted worthy to suffer for his Lord.

Paul, whose Christian life began in prayer, continued to be a man of God who was characterized in a special way with a heart that sought God's best for his friends and for himself. His heart is especially revealed to us in and through his prayers.

As we consider Paul, the Man of Prayer, it is my hope that we will also learn to pray with Paul's confidence and insights into God's purpose for us and those for whom we intercede.

Prayer Principle #1

Paul's example demonstrates clearly that prayer is essential if we are to understand the experiences with God which we may have had. His experience on the Damascus road and his prayers during the three days of blindness brought him into a new living and personal relationship with God through Jesus the Messiah.

1. How has Jesus changed your conception of God?

2. In what ways has your faith in Jesus shaped how you pray?

3. What is prayer to you? For you, is prayer a duty, an emergency appeal, or something that brings you into a more intimate relationship with God?

4. What can we do to bring a new aliveness to our times of prayer?

PART ONE

PAUL'S PRACTICE OF PRAYER

1. Discipline and Habit

Because of his background we should expect to find in Paul's practice of prayer a strong indication of discipline of habit. After all he was a Pharisee and though he no longer was seeking to impress God, he knew that he needed the grace of God -- and the demands of grace and love are surely not lower than the demands of the law. The habits which we establish free us from the necessity of consciously thinking and deciding. If we had to consciously decide and concentrate each time we tied our shoes it would be a chore, but as it is we can do it without thinking. If we make it a habit to pray first thing in the morning, we enter into a spirit of prayer before we even begin to do it.

When one looks for evidence of "habit" in Paul's practice of prayer, it is seen in at least two facets of his life.

1. His statements that he always remembers them in his prayers and the like are evidence that Paul continued the regular times for prayer which he had established as a Pharisee. However, it was not only Paul, the early Christians seem to have continued the times for prayer familiar to every Jew. One needs only to note the times which Luke specified in Acts: 9:00 a.m. -- the time when the Holy Spirit fell on the disciples on the day of Pentecost (Acts 2:15); 3:00 p.m. -- the healing of the cripple (Acts 3:1 *One day Peter and John were going up to the temple at the time of prayer--at three in the afternoon),* it was also the time when the centurion Cornelius had his vision to send for Peter (Acts 10:3); and 12:00 noon, the time

when Peter had gone up on the roof to meditate and pray while he waited for lunch (Acts 10:9). What is significant about these times is that 9:00, 12:00, and 3:00 were the set times for prayer for the pious in Israel. These times were important because 9:00 a.m. and 3:00 p.m. were the times for the morning and evening sacrifice at the Jerusalem Temple. It was not unusual for prayers to also be made before retiring for the day.

So how did Paul find time to "remember" all his churches and friends in prayer? He kept the hours of prayer. How much more praying would we do for our family and friends, the world and the things of the Kingdom if we kept three set times for prayer each day.

2. We find Paul in the book of Acts, always going to the synagogue on the Sabbath. This was not just a missionary strategy, though it is certainly Paul's intention to preach first to those who had understanding and belief in the Scriptures, the Synagogue service was above all a time for prayer. Regularly attending a service of worship, praying in a communal setting, was intensely important for Paul himself and a practice that he instituted in all the churches he founded. Although the day of worship gradually changed from the seventh day to the first day of the week in celebration of the resurrection of Jesus (1 Corinthians 16:2) it is significant that the seven day interval was maintained. There is no reason that a week consists of seven days, except that God commanded, *Remember the Sabbath day to keep it holy..."* (Exodus 20:8), which reflects God's creation of the world in seven days.

Paul's practice of prayer contained several facets which appear to be integral to his prayer habit.

2. Thanksgiving and Praise

One cannot read Paul's letters without being struck by the preponderance of statements that reflect his gratitude and praise to God. This is not just some literary technique which Paul employs but seems to reflect the mental-spiritual tenor of his spirituality.

Although the normal form for a Greek letter included an expressed thanksgiving for the recipient or something the receiver has done, Paul's thanksgivings are generally more extended and in some of the letters even contain a summary of the contents of the letter.

For Paul, the thanksgivings were an opportunity for him to praise God for what the Lord was doing in the lives of the addressees. It was a chance for Paul to commend and encourage them because of their faithfulness, work, love for one another etc. All of this was evidence of the grace of God which was active in them as individuals and in the church as a whole. With the exception of Philippians 4:10-18, his thanksgivings are never "personal," in the sense of acknowledgement of something which the recipients had done for him, but always couched in terms that describe what God was doing among them.

Throughout his letters Paul often expresses thanks and praise for what God has done and for who God is. His praise and gratitude are not at all grounded in the circumstances of his life for we find him and Silas in prison in Philippi, singing and praising God at midnight (Acts 16) and Paul's prison letters are some of the most joyous of his writings.

What is the source of this joy? I think we find it in Paul's absolute and deep abandonment of himself to God and to obedience to God's will. This certainty of God and the belief that God has a purpose for him to accomplish means for Paul that he can live in the reality of the present moment. God is involved in what is happening to him at any moment, and although Satan is active in opposition, Paul's task is to do what needs to be done to the glory of God, to be faithful, and clear in his witness. To use his language of prayer for the Colossians, Paul's commitment is *"to live a life worthy of the Lord and to please him in every way"* (Colossians 1:10).

When one adopts the perspective that this present moment is God's moment for me there comes a sense of expectancy. Although I may not always know what he is up to, because I am in tune with him and seeking to be faithful to whatever he calls me to do, I can dare to relax and look for the evidence of God's goodness and direction. When we look for it, we will inevitably see the goodness of the Lord.

To begin to live in God's moment means that we are free to live life to the full. To live in God's moment frees us from the preoccupation with ourselves. We can forget ourselves and reach out and serve others, focus on the tasks we need to do, and "*do it all in the name of the Lord Jesus giving thanks to God the Father through him*" (Colossians 3:17). When we enjoy nature, our work, interaction with others, family and friends; when we rise to the challenges which face us and give our best effort to whatever we are doing, we bring joy to the heart of God. Just as parents experience deep satisfaction and joy when their children enjoy the gifts they have given them, so God knows joy when we enjoy his gifts. We can live in the present and celebrate what is happening now, rather than borrowing problems from the future or living with regrets for the past. It is God's time all the time, and we live in his presencc. As the Psalmist expressed it: *This is the day that Lord has made, let us rejoice and be glad in it* (Psalm 118:24).

It has often been observed that two common Greek words for time *kairos* and *chronos* catch this idea: *chronos* emphasis the passing of time and *kairos* emphasizes the significance of the moment. *Carpos Diem, seize the day!* Or as Paul put it Ephesians 5:15-17, *Be very careful, then, how you live--not as unwise but as wise, making the most of every opportunity, because the days are evil. Therefore do not be foolish, but understand what the Lord's will is.*

Paul's life and prayers reflect the joyous gratitude for God's faithfulness and goodness. His thankfulness and praise to God touch every facet of his life--both the good and the difficult.

3. Paul Prayed For Others And Requested Prayer For Himself

Paul prayed for others. This, of course, is the most obvious aspect of the prayers in his letters. Paul believed that prayer was important and that it made a difference, both in one's own life and also in the life of others. Prayer was not some theoretical teaching for Paul, it was the very heart of his relationship with God through Christ and the very essence of his service for his Lord. Prayer is the gift which God has given us that enables us to release the power of the Spirit into the lives of those for whom we pray. Prayer enables us to participate in God's work and is one of the ways that God's work gets done in the world. I think it was John Wesley who once observed, "There are some things that God will not do if we do not pray."

It might be interesting to note that Paul not only prayed for others but also asked others to pray for him. He did not regard himself as some spiritual giant who was above needing the assistance of others. His requests for prayer also give us a hint that these requests also formed part of his prayers for himself.

His requests are often that it will be God's will for him to visit his friends to whom he is writing. And at times that God would open the door for effective witness. He asks that they pray that he might be rescued from the plots of wicked men who oppose the gospel. He also asks the recipients to remember his chains, that is, to pray that he might be released from prison.

One theme that runs through many of the requests for prayer that Paul makes is quite interesting -- for it shows the frailty of this giant of faith. He asks that others pray for his courage, steadfastness, and clarity of thought and expression when he stands before those who oppose the gospel or the tribunals before whom he had to give an account. The very fact that he makes this request so often indicates how fearful Paul was and how great the temptation must have been to save his own skin rather than bear firm and clear witness to his Lord and the gospel. The need for courage and the temptations contained in his trials are quite evident when one reads the list of what he endured in 2 Corinthians 11:23-29 or his wonderful statement of contrasts in 2 Corinthians 4:7-11: *But we have this treasure in jars of clay to show that this all-surpassing power is from God and not from us. We are hard pressed on every side, but not crushed; perplexed, but not in despair; persecuted, but not abandoned; struck down, but not destroyed. We always carry around in our body the death of Jesus, so that the life of Jesus may also be revealed in our body. For we who are alive are always being given over to death for Jesus' sake, so that his life may be revealed in our mortal body.*

It is easy to be courageous when there is no opposition, and have we not all had the frustrating experience of knowing what we should have said after the opportunity to say it was past! Paul is aware enough of his own human weakness to ask for prayer that he might be adequate to the challenges he faced. There is a strength which we receive from the assurance that others are lifting us up to God. Paul describes his own prayer for the Colossians: *I want you to know how much I am struggling for you and for those at Laodicea, and for all who have not met me personally. My purpose is that they may be encouraged in heart and united in love, so that they may have the full riches of complete understanding...* (Colossians 2:1-2). Through prayer we can bring God's grace and power to bear upon the struggles others are experiencing. Prayer is one of the ways that God has given us to participate in the great redemptive love of Christ.

Paul's sense of responsibility for the churches weighed heavily upon him. At the conclusion of a list of things he had suffered as a result of his obedience to God's call he writes, *Besides everything else, I have the daily burden because of my anxiety about all the churches* (2 Corinthians 11:28). We can assume that this concern moved Paul to pray with great intensity for the churches.

For Paul, to be the apostle to the Gentiles meant that he was called to take the gospel and found churches where the good news of Jesus Christ had not yet reached. Thus he writes to the Romans, *my one ambition is to proclaim the gospel where the name of Christ is not known, lest I build on someone else's foundation* (Romans 15:20). This passion involved great hardship and opposition, so it is not surprising that Paul asked for prayer and we can assume it was also a strong component of his personal prayers: *Finally, brothers, pray for us--that the word of the Lord may spread rapidly, and that it may be honored the way it is among you. Also pray that we may be rescued from worthless and evil people, since not everyone holds to the faith* (2 Thessalonians 3:1-2). Even later in his ministry when he is imprisoned this passion to share the gospel clearly and with boldness remains: *At the same time pray for us--that God would open before us a door for the word so that we may tell the secret about Christ, for which I have been imprisoned. May I reveal it as clearly as I should* (Colossians 4:3-4, see also Ephesians 6:19-20). When he requests prayer that he might be released from prison, it is not simply for his own safety and comfort but so that he might be free to continue his mission to reach the unreached for Christ and to care for the churches (see Philippians 1:12-13,15-25).

Paul's care and concern for the churches is reflected in the letters he writes. Paul is responsible for developing a new form of literature -- letters. Although letters were written before and there was even a somewhat standard form that writers used, Paul is the first person to use letters so extensively. Although there was no public mail system, travel was relatively safe and Paul used couriers, usually friends and associates, to deliver his letters to the various churches. These letters along with the personal emissaries enabled Paul to maintain connection with his churches even though he was separated by many miles from them.

In his letters Paul addresses some of his concerns about the church and gives instructions to help the recipients to grow in their understanding of the gospel and the life-style that commitment to Jesus Christ as Lord demanded. These letters often included a summary of prayers he prayed for them. A cursory look at these prayer reports show that Paul is not concerned about their physical safety or protection from persecution, but rather about their relationship with Christ and their practical expressions of their faith in Christ as they lived in an ungodly world.

One of the things that characterize Paul's letters and set them apart from the other letters in the New Testament[5] is that he not only tells the recipients that he prays for them but also gives a sketch of what it is he is praying. There are really three different categories of prayers which are involved as we consider Paul's prayers for others: prayer reports, wish prayers, and intercessions. We will consider each category.

The Prayer Reports

The "prayer reports" occur six times in his letters and comprise what most people think of when the prayers of Paul are considered. It should be observed that these prayer reports are not necessarily the actual words he prayed, but rather the subject matter and thrust of his prayers. I am going to resist the temptation to do an exposition of the prayer reports in Paul's letters. One can find this in any good commentary and there are several books that expand on the meaning and significance of these prayers.[6] I would, however, like to make a few observations.

1. These prayers are for groups of people -- the church, and not for individuals. Therefore:

- Paul does not pray about the health issues of particular people.

- Nor does he pray about the situation these Christians are facing. Although he knows they are facing opposition and persecution, Paul does not pray for their safety or protection. This, of course, does not mean that he did not pray for these things, for he asks the Roman church to pray for his safety (Romans 15:30-31).

- Paul's prayer reports are concerned with the kingdom of God and the spiritual vitality and health of the church. What he prays for the church, however, also has specific application for each person, for unless individuals are spiritually vital the church cannot be a vital and attractive force in a pagan world or bring glory to God.

- As Paul prays for the church he is standing in the Biblical tradition which emphasizes the solidarity of the people of God, which is also the focus of the prayer of the Eighteen Benedictions. We who have been shaped by the individualistic self-understanding of the American frontier, tend to read Paul through the lens of the solitary individual. The glory of God is seen, however, not merely in an individual's relationship with God but in the life of the community of the faithful followers of Christ. It is in the midst of community that love becomes a motivating force and the transforming power of Christ is made evident.

Paul, of course, is aware and concerned for individuals as well as the whole group. He refers to individuals as "saints", and gives the names of numerous people in his letters. However, his concern in his prayers seems to be that which will make Christians vital and bring unity to the church.

Why is the unity of the church so important to Paul?[7] It is not merely a pragmatic concern, but a theological concern. As Paul asks in 1 Corinthians 1:13, *Is Christ divided? Was Paul crucified for you? Were you baptized in the name of Paul?* When one considers the metaphors or pictures which Paul used to describe the church, they mostly refer to Christians in a collective sense and cannot be meaningfully applied to just an individual.[8]

Just as Israel is viewed in a collective sense in the Old Testament, so

Paul views the church in a collective sense. The church is now the people of God, thus Paul can write: *we are the true circumcision,* i.e., the true people of God (Philippians 3:3). But as Romans 9-11 shows us, the church has not replaced Israel but rather has been grafted onto the olive tree and is to be considered as part of the true Israel. Believing Gentiles, then, are considered as the children of Abraham (see Galatians 3:14, 26-29) and as spiritual Jews possessing the circumcision of the heart (Romans 2:28-29).

When Paul indicates that he prays that they may know *the riches of his [God's] glorious inheritance in the saints* (Ephesians 1:18), he is picking up a refrain often found in the Old Testament. In fact, this refrain is the underpinning of all the promises to Israel of blessing--both spiritual and material, and also of the warnings and judgments. The first statement of this refrain is found in Exodus 19:5-6, *Now if you obey me fully and keep my covenant, then out of all the nations you will be my treasured possession. Although the whole earth is mine, you will be for me a kingdom of priests and a holy nation.*

Numerous times in the Old Testament Israel is called God's portion or inheritance. God takes a special delight in the people whom he has chosen. It is through his people that God's glory is displayed to the world. However, when his people are disobedient and rebellious they bring dishonor to God. As Ezekiel 36:22-23 puts it, *Therefore say to the house of Israel, 'This is what the Sovereign Lord says: It is not for your sake, O house of Israel, that I am going to do these things, but for the sake of my holy name, which you have profaned among the nations where you have gone. I will show the holiness of my great name, which has been profaned among the nations, the name you have profaned among them...*

Paul wants the readers of his letter to realize that their faith in Christ that brings them into God's family gives great joy to the Father (see Zephaniah 3:17) and that he delights to bless them so that they are "more than conquerors" in the face of all the opposition of the forces of evil. His prayers aim at the things that would enable them to bring glory to God and keep them from bringing dishonor to their heavenly Father.

2. When the prayer reports themselves are considered carefully it becomes clear that they consist of both primary and secondary

requests. The primary requests are always for something central to the Christian life; usually for something which only God could do and which will bring glory to God. The secondary requests spell out what the results will be to the believers as the primary request is fulfilled. To put it another way, the secondary requests state the beneficial results which will come as a by-product of the primary request.

1 Thessalonians 3:12-13 contains two primary requests and a result.

Primary: *May the Lord make your love increase and overflow for each other and for everyone else...May he strengthen your hearts so that*

Secondary: *You will be blameless and holy in the presence of our God and Father when the Lord Jesus comes...*

Although in its form, this is really a wish prayer. It is more complex than most wish prayers and in its structure it follows the pattern of the prayer reports.

2 Thessalonians 1:11-12 contains two primary and one secondary request.

Primary: *I pray that our God may count you worthy of his calling, and that by his power he may fulfill every good purpose of yours and every act prompted by your faith.*

Secondary: *We pray this so that the name of our Lord Jesus may be glorified in you and you in him, according to the grace of our God and the Lord Jesus Christ.*

Ephesians 1:17-20 contains two primary requests and three or four secondary ones.

Primary: *I pray that God would give you the Spirit of wisdom and revelation so that you may know him better. I pray that the eyes of your heart may be enlightened in order that*

Secondary: *You may know the hope to which he has called you;*

- (you may know) *the riches of his glorious inheritance in the saints;*
- (you may know) *the incomparably great power for us who believe...*
- (you may know) that Jesus Christ is Lord of all [implied in the verses that follow].

Ephesians 3:16-19 contains two primary requests and four secondary ones

Primary: *I pray that...he may strengthen you with power through his Spirit in your inner being;* (v. 16) *That you may be filled to the measure of all the fullness of God.* (v.19)

Secondary: *So that Christ may dwell in your hearts through faith:*

- *That you* [may be], *rooted and grounded in love*
- *May have power, together with all the saints, to grasp how wide and long and high and deep is the love of Christ,*
- *And to know this love that surpasses knowledge.*

The doxology that concludes the prayer emphasizes that it is all about God and that he is able to do what seems impossible.

Philippians 1:9-11 contains two primary requests with three secondary ones.

Primary: *That your love may abound more and more in knowledge and depth of insight, (v. 9)* And [that your lives may bring] *glory and praise to God. (v. 11)*

Secondary: *So that you can discern what is best*

- *And may be pure and blameless until the day of Christ*
- *Filled with the fruit of righteous that come through Jesus Christ*

Colossians 1:9-12 contain two primary requests and six secondary ones.

Primary: *Asking God to fill you with the knowledge of his will through all spiritual wisdom and understanding so that you may live a life worthy of the Lord and may please him in every way*

Secondary: *Bearing fruit in every good work;*

- *Growing in the knowledge of God;*
- *Being strengthened with all power…*
- *So that you may have great endurance and patience,*
- *And joyfully give thanks to the Father who has qualified you to share in the inheritance of the saints in the kingdom of light.*

Paul's concern for the church drives him to intense prayer. The prayer reports show something of what Paul meant when he wrote, *Besides everything else, I face daily the pressure of my concern for all the churches. Who is weak, and I do not feel weak? Who is led into sin, and I do not inwardly burn?* (2 Corinthians 11:28-29). Paul knows that they are engaged in a spiritual battle which is against the very forces of evil (see Ephesians 6:10-18) and his intense prayer and concern is *that Satan might not outwit us. For we are not unaware of his schemes* (2 Corinthians 2:11).

Paul's passion for these new Christians is stated in 2 Corinthians 11:2-3: *I am jealous for you with a godly jealousy. I promised you to one husband, to Christ, so that I might present you as a pure virgin to him. I am afraid that just as Eve was deceived by the serpent's cunning, your minds may somehow be led astray from your sincere and pure devotion to Christ.* Paul states it again in Colossians 2:1-2, *I want you to know how much I am struggling for you and for those at Laodicea, and for all who have not met me personally. My purpose is that they may be encouraged in heart and united in love, so that they may have the full riches of complete understanding, in order that they may know the mystery of God, namely,*

Christ, in whom are hidden all the treasures of wisdom and knowledge.[9]

The prayer reports express in deep emotional tones the passion which Paul had that he might present every person, for whom he has any responsibility, complete and mature to Christ Jesus his Lord.[10] They are his crown and glory when he stands to give an account of himself.[11] Paul's heart cry is also that of every pastor and, yes, of every Christian parent for their children.

Prayer Principle #2

Pray for the things relating to spiritual life and not just about difficult life situations.

Paul's prayer reports show that he had a passion for the unity and spiritual growth of those who believe in Jesus -- for he understood the schemes of Satan. Although he was aware of problems, Paul's prayer reports are always positive and never negative in tone.

Do you find it easier to prayer against the weakness and evil in the church, world, or friends? How would your prayers change if you focused on what you sense that God desired for others?

1. Create your own prayer report on how you might pray for your church or the group of believers with which you identify.

Primary: Prayer request

Secondary: Prayer requests (or things which would result as the primary prayer is fulfilled)

2. How might you pray for your family and loved ones

The Wish Prayers

While it is generally assumed that Paul only gives us reports of his prayers and not the actual prayers themselves, there is another class of prayers, which we designate as "wish prayers", which may come very close to being the actual words that Paul used in prayer. There are nine such prayers in Paul's letters.

In form, the wish prayer generally begins with "May the Lord" or

"May God." They are usually short and simple, which also makes them memorable. A wish prayer just seems to pop up in the midst of his letters and show us that prayer was not reserved by Paul for the more formal or extended times of prayer. Paul could break into a short prayer and then continue with his work or writing without there being any break. Eight of the nine wish prayers are essentially a statement of blessing.

There is a certain air of confident joyfulness in these prayers that reflect the spirit of one who is sure that God delights to bless his children, and has himself experienced these blessings. As one reads these wish prayers some of the great statements of affirmation which occur in Paul's letters can be heard, such as: *My God will meet all your needs according to his glorious riches in Christ Jesus* (Philippians 4:19); or *he who began a good work in you will bring it to completion...* (Philippians 1:6); or *...hope does not disappoint us, because God has poured out his love into our hearts by the Holy Spirit, whom he has given us* (Romans 5:4-5). Because of the simplicity and straightforwardness of the wish prayers they really do not need to be explained.

May the God who gives endurance and encouragement give you a spirit of unity among yourselves as you follow Christ Jesus, so that with one heart and mouth you may glorify the God and Father of our Lord Jesus Christ. Romans 15:5-6

May the God of hope fill you with all joy and peace as you trust in him, so that you may overflow with hope by the power of the Holy Spirit. Romans 15:13

Now we pray to God that you will not do anything wrong. Not that people will see that we have stood the test but that you will do what is right even though we may seem to have failed. 2 Corinthians 13:7

May the Lord make your love increase and overflow for each other and for everyone else, just as ours does for you. May he strengthen your hearts so that you will be blameless and holy in the presence of our God and Father when our Lord Jesus comes with all his holy ones. 1 Thessalonians 3:12-13

May God himself, the God of peace, sanctify you through and through. May your whole spirit, soul and body be kept blameless at the coming of our Lord Jesus Christ. The one who calls you is faithful and he will do it. 1 Thessalonians 5:23-24

May the Lord Jesus Christ himself and God our Father, who loved us and by his grace gave us eternal encouragement and good hope, encourage your hearts and strengthen you in every good deed and word. 2 Thessalonians 2:16-17

May the Lord direct your hearts into God's love and Christ's perseverance. 2 Thessalonians 3:5

Now may the Lord of peace himself give you peace at all times and in every way. The Lord be with all of you. 2 Thessalonians 3:16

These prayer wishes are in a real sense prayer blessings in which the Apostle prayers for the endowment of some fruit of the Spirit to be reinforced within the community of believers.

PAULINE PRAYER PRINCIPLE #3

Through prayer, we can bless others.

As Paul thought about different groups of believers, he was often impressed to pray a prayer blessing -- which was a Jewish custom -- for them. In each case his prayer wish is that they might be blessed with the increase of a fruit of the Spirit so that individually and as a group they might become more Christ-like. Their testimony and impact on the unbelieving society would thus be more effective.

What fruit of the Spirit (see Galatians 5:22-23) needs to be increased in yourself? Your faith community? Your family?

Write a wish prayer of blessing for each of the above. Make it personal and if appropriate, share it with those you wish to bless.

The Prayers of Intercession

There is another class of prayers in Paul's letters which I have called intercessions.

The Webster's New World Dictionary defines the word intercede: "to plead or make a request in behalf of another or others." In a sense all Paul's prayers for others are then intercessory. However , I am using the term in a more restricted sense to describe the prayers which are more mediatory in nature and often more intense than other types of prayers. The intercessory prayers in Paul are of three types: for individuals; another is for the salvation of Israel, and the third type comes as a result of his care for the churches. In the next section we will deal with the last two types.

Paul only refers to his prayers for specific people two times in his letters. In his letter to Philemon it is prayer of encouragement and affirmation for one who had been a faithful friend: *I pray that you may be active in sharing your faith, so you will have full understanding of every good thing we have in Christ. Your love has given me great joy and encouragement, because you, brother, have refreshed the hearts of the saints (6-7).*

In 2 Timothy Paul reveals how deeply he was hurt by being deserted at a time he really needed support, for he mentions it twice, and prays specifically for Onesiphorus. It is interesting that in 4:19 he sends greetings to the household of Onesiphorus.

At my first defense, no one came to my support, but every one deserted me. May it not be held against them (4:16). In the first chapter he writes: *You know that everyone in the province of Asia has deserted me, including Phygelus and Hermogenes. May the Lord show mercy on the household of Onesiphorus, because he often refreshed me and was not ashamed of my chains...May the Lord grant that he will find mercy from the Lord on that day! You know very well in how many ways he helped me in Ephesus* (1:15-18). Paul asks for mercy and forgiveness on those who had deserted him. He not only preached that we must forgive others but practiced forgiveness himself.

4. PAUL'S CARE FOR THE CHURCHES

Paul's oversight and care for the churches weighed heavily upon him. At the conclusion of a list of things he had suffered as a result of his obedience to God's call, he writes, *Besides everything else, I have the daily burden because of my anxiety about all the churches* (2 Corinthians 11:28).

The converts in the churches which Paul founded came from three different kinds of people. Paul followed the principle that the gospel was *first for the Jew, then for the Gentile* (Romans 1:16); thus he always began his mission work in a new city at the synagogue if there was one. As a result of his preaching in the synagogue there would be some Jews who believed. These would have been raised on the teaching of the Torah and the stories of God's dealing with Israel. In the synagogue there would also be some Gentiles who had been attracted to Judaism by its high morality and strong faith in God and their disillusionment with the popular religion and the pagan gods. Some of these may have been full converts to Judaism, known as proselytes, and others were simply interested parties, known as God-fearers. It can be assumed that these Gentiles would share the faith in one God and the fundamental ethical teachings of the Old Testament. When persecution broke out and Paul had to leave the synagogue, the preaching would be to pagans. Thus the third kind of persons who made up the church would be Gentiles who came directly out of paganism and who had little understanding of the God of Abraham, Isaac and Jacob and no knowledge of Judaism. Making the situation even more complex was the various economic and social classes involved: educated and uneducated, slave owners and slaves, some from the more wealthy and those from the lower classes (see 1 Corinthians 1:26). It is thus no wonder that Paul was concerned about the unity of the churches and their understanding of the gospel. This also explains his philosophy of evangelism in 1 Corinthians 9:19-23.

> *I make myself a slave to everyone, to win as many as possible...I have become all things to all men so that by all possible means I might save some (I Corinthians 9:19,22).*

Paul's concern for the churches was not a dispassionate concern. He writes to the Colossians, *For I want you to know how much I struggle for you, and for those in Loadicea and for all who have never seen me face to face. Because they are united in love, I pray...* (Colossians 2:1-2); he writes of Epaphras, *He is always wrestling in pray for you* (Colossians 4:12). The words translated "struggle" and "wrestling" are words from which we get the words "agony and agonize" and reflect that in their prayers Paul and Ephaphras are engaged in a spiritual warfare with the very forces of evil. This intercessory prayer was not just a pleasant pass time, they were fighting the spiritual forces that would destroy the faith of these new Christians. At the same time through their faith and prayers Paul and Epaphras were releasing the resources of the Holy Spirit who is able to help these believers to stand firm and to grow in their understanding of Christ and salvation.

This kind of intercessory prayer is more than simply prayer for someone else. It is a prayer that demands the intercessor to pay a cost in at least three dimensions.

First, it demands the death to self. It is such a deep submission to Christ that one shares the heart and desires of Christ for those prayed for. There is no longer room for self-interest. When Paul writes in Galatians 2:20, *I have been crucified with Christ ...* he means more than that he has died with Christ in the sense that he considers himself dead to sin and alive to God in Christ Jesus (Romans 6:11). There is another dimension, a dying to self that involves such a submission to our Lord that our own comfort is unimportant and our possessions are his to use as he directs.

Second, it involves an identification in Christ's love with those for whom we intercede. Rees Howells, the great Welsh intercessor, said "This is the law of intercession on every level of life: that only so far as we have been tested and proved willing to do a thing ourselves can we intercede for others. Christ is our Intercessor because He took the place of each one prayed for." [12]

Intercessory prayer involves one standing in the gap on behalf of another. Sometimes this involves great emotion. We see this in the Apostle Paul when he records, *Brothers, my heart's desire and prayer to God for the Israelites is that they may be saved.* (Romans 10:1). *I speak the truth in Christ -- I am not lying, my conscience confirms it in the Holy Spirit -- I have great sorrow and unceasing anguish in my heart. For I could wish that I myself were cursed and cut off from Christ for the sake of my brothers, those of my own race, the people of Israel* (Romans 9:1-4).

Prayer Principles #4

We need to be involved with meaningful intercessory prayer for those who do not know our Savior.

In an update in a newsletter from Pioneers: Be encouraged by these words from a Pioneers leader in South Asia, "If the work we have been called to accomplish among the unreached is essentially a spiritual calling with eternal consequences, then we dare not neglect the most sacred privilege of prayer…People of prayer are the ones who change the world, bringing hope to those lost in darkness…Our great challenge is to grasp the radical implications of a life of prayer, to see objectively the devastating consequences of neglecting so great a responsibility, and to know the passion of His Spirit leading us into intimacy with Him."

Pioneers, TEAM EPAPHRAS NEWS, July 10, 2010

Make list of people you know who are in need of discovering God's love in Jesus Christ, for whom you can begin to pray.

Expand your list to include at least one missionary, a country or people group and a social agency that is seeking to help the poor and suffering people of the world.

Sometimes a prayer list can become overwhelming and thus a detriment to prayer. Divide you list so that you pray for some on Monday, some on Tuesday, etc. so that each week each of those on your list will be prayed for.

5. PAUL PRAYED FOR HIMSELF, Part I

Only two times in his letters does Paul directly mention his prayers for himself. In Romans 15:30-31 he asks the church in Rome *to join in my struggle by praying to God for me…* His struggle surely included earnest, intense prayer. Unbelieving Jews had already attempted to kill him (Acts 9:29-30). Paul could tell the Ephesian elders: *And now compelled by the Spirit, I am going to Jerusalem, not knowing what will happen to me there. I only know that in every city the Holy Spirit warns me that prison and hardships are facing me. However, I consider my life worth nothing to me, if only I may finish the race and complete the task the Lord Jesus has given me--the task of testifying to the gospel* (Acts 20:22-24). Acts 23:12-22 shows that his anxiety was well founded, for the hatred against him was strong. Paul is sustained by the prayers of God's people.

The second mention which Paul makes of a prayer for himself is 2 Corinthians 12:7-10.

> *To keep me from becoming conceited because of these surpassingly great revelations, there was given to me a thorn in my flesh, a messenger of Satan, to torment me. Three times I pleaded with the Lord to take it away from me. But he said to me, 'My grace is sufficient for you, for my power is made perfect in weakness.' Therefore I will boast all the more gladly about my weaknesses, so that Christ's power may rest on me. That is why, for Christ's sake, I delight in weaknesses, in insults, in hardships, in persecutions, in difficulties. For when I am weak, then I am strong.*

This is an interesting passage when considered in the context of prayer. Paul says that he was given a thorn in the flesh to keep him from becoming too conceited. He calls this thorn, "a messenger of Satan," sent to "torment me."

This is the nearest example in the New Testament of the experience of Job, the great sufferer in the Old Testament. Satan, the tormenter, was given permission to test Job, even though he was a righteous man. Paul says that a thorn in the flesh was given him and just as in the Old Testament example, God seems to approve of this messenger of Satan. Paul's explanation is that this was to keep him from being overly elated and boastful about his visionary experiences. Satan seems to be cast in the role of doing that which fulfills God's purpose.

Even in the temptations of Jesus we are informed that *Jesus was led by the Spirit into the desert to be tempted by the devil* (Matthew 4:1). Satan, in the mysterious sovereignty of God, seems to become an agent to accomplish God's purpose. Perhaps this is an example of Romans 8:28: *And we know that in all things God works for the good of those who love him, who have been called according to his purpose.*

What the thorn in the flesh was is matter of conjecture. Most scholars believe it was some kind of physical ailment which made it difficult for Paul to do the missionary work to which he had been assigned. Although Paul prayed that the thorn might be removed, and he says he prayed three times, the Lord refused his request and in place of the healing gives the promise that *my grace is sufficient for you, for my strength is made perfect in weakness.* The three times may be a traditional way of saying that he often prayed for healing until the Lord gave him the promise.[13]

Paul's response to the answer "no', and the promise of the Lord, shows the deep abandonment which he had made to the will of the Lord. He does not whine but rather turns the "thorn in the flesh" into a way for him to praise the Lord and to draw upon the strength of the promise given him. The Greek word translated "boast" could also be translated "rejoice." This is the same resilient, positive attitude which he had when he penned Philippians 1:12-26.

This episode from Paul's own life has been a source of inspiration to many. What is our response to be when God seems to say "no" to our most ardent prayers for healing. My wife, Margaret, faced this as she battled with ovarian cancer, which after a 12 year battle finally took her life. She did not know why God did not heal her. However, she adopted Paul's attitude of praise and submission to the Lord, with a commitment to serve him as best she could with the strength he gave her. As a result, not only was she given the ability to enjoy the quality of life she had, but she became an inspiration and encouragement to an amazing assortment of people who were also struggling with deep hurts or also a terminal illness. As Paul wrote in 2 Corinthians 1:5 *...through Christ our comfort overflows.*

There are several lessons of prayer that are illustrated by the experience of Paul.

1. It is right and natural to pray about our health and the health of others. Sometimes, as in the case of Epaphroditus (Philippians 2:25-30), the prayer results in healing. As Paul says, *God had mercy on him and not on him only but also on me, to spare me sorrow upon sorrow* (Phil. 2:27). But sometimes he says "no."

2. Although one may be righteous and holy and committed to serving God, prayer remains a mystery. Prayer is not a means of pressuring or forcing God to do our will. Prayer is not a magical incantation which, if the right words are said with enough intensity and emotion, then God will have to act. Rather prayer is one of the means by which God has provided for us to communicate with him. Prayer has more to do with our relationship with God than simply getting "answers." At times we are guilty of seeking God's gifts rather than God himself. We need to "seek his face, not just his hand."[14]

3. It is important to note that the Lord responds to Paul's prayer. What Paul desires is important to God and the Lord responds to his request with the promise of his grace. The Lord does not treat Paul as a pawn but communicates to Paul that He has a purpose different from that which Paul expected.

In any interaction, whether between two people or between you and God, there is reciprocal relationship. What one thinks and says is important to the other one. It is incorrect for us to believe that somehow God has already predetermined what will happen. If that were the case then prayer would be an exercise in futility and nothing we pray would change the outcome which God has already predetermined would take place. But this is obviously not true. What we do can change what God does. There are many examples in the Old Testament, (i.e., the many blessing and cursing statements: 'if you do this I will do this, but if you do that I will do that'). The future is not already determined but God adjusts his response according to our obedience or disobedience. In the New Testament we find Peter writing, *It is not the will of your Father that any should perish but that all should come to repentance* (2 Peter 3:9). If one rejects Christ, there is a sure result, and if one accepts Christ the result is also certain. *The wages of sin is death but the gift of God is eternal life in Christ Jesus our Lord.* (Romans 6:23).

4. A "no" to our prayer, or as some would put it, to have our prayer

unanswered, is not in and of itself, evidence of God's displeasure. Remember Gethsemane and think about Paul's thorn in the flesh. God has purposes greater than our ability to perceive (see Isaiah 55:8). With the help of the Lord it is possible for us to turn the negative into a positive.

5. The attitude we choose to take when we do not get the answer we wish, indicates the depth of our commitment and relationship with God. It also will determine the value our suffering has for others as well as in the cultivating of our own character toward holiness. "Character determines how a [person] interprets God's will." [15]

Paul's response to the Lord's promise was, *Therefore I will boast all the more gladly about my weaknesses, so that Christ's power may rest on me. That is why, for Christ's sake, I delight in hardships, in persecution, in difficulties. For when I am weak, then I am strong* (2 Corinthians 12:9b-10). The word translated "boast" can also mean rejoice. Paul deliberately chooses to rejoice rather than complain about his "weaknesses." His attitude and trust in Christ enabled that which was bad, "the messenger of Satan," to be transformed into that which glorified Christ and empowered Paul to continue to be the encourager and blessing to others.

Oswald Chambers made some observations that are pertinent to what we have been saying.

"If we are going to be used by God, He will take us through a multitude of experiences that are not meant for us at all, but meant to make us useful in His hands. There are things we go through which are unexplainable on any other line, and the nearer we get to God the more inexplicable the way seems. It is only on looking back and by getting an explanation from God's Word that we understand His dealings with us." [16]

"Not only does God waste His saints according to the judgments of men, He seems to bruise them most mercilessly. You say, 'But it could never be God's will to bruise me': if it pleased the Lord to bruise His own Son, why should He not bruise you? To choose suffering is a disease; but to choose God's will even though it means suffering is to suffer as Jesus did-- 'according to the will of God'.

In the Bible it is never the idealizing of the sufferer that is brought out, but the glorifying of God. God always serves Himself out of the saint's personal experience of suffering." [17]

PRAYER PRINCIPLE # 5

Our prayers are not always answered in the way we had desired.

Paul discovered that prayer is not a *carte blanch check* where we always get what we wish. God remains Sovereign and as Isaiah 55:8-9 tell us, his ways are not always our ways. Sooner or later we must surrender to the divine will, just as Jesus did in the Garden of Gethsemane.

Our Lord was especially gracious to Paul, for he gave him a clear word and the promise that *my grace is sufficient for you.* When Paul understood this it changed his stance from asking to surrender and rejoicing in his "thorn in the flesh."

In what ways has the Lord denied a prayer answer that you had desired? What affect did the denial have upon you? How did you respond?

How did the Lord bring his grace into your situation? Did you receive a special promise that sustained you?

Have you ever experienced Romans 8:28 – God bringing good out of the bad? Give an example.

6. PAUL'S PRAYERS FOR HIMSELF, Part II

When one considers what Paul prayed for himself, he must be careful for Paul seldom mentions directly what he prayed for. So our investigation will of necessity be focused on things that concerned him from which we can infer something of the content of his prayers for himself. When Paul asked the churches to pray about something we can assume he is also praying about that. When a personal reference is mentioned several times, we may assume that this also comprised a component of his prayers for himself.

Paul's Call and Appointment

Paul lived with a vivid sense of God's call on his life to be the Apostle to the Gentiles. For Paul the call to faith in Christ Jesus and his appointment to be the Apostle to the Gentiles is one call. Although it is one call, it has two aspects: A call to faith in Christ and salvation and the call to be an apostle.

Paul does not often refer specifically to his conversion experience, and never gives details about his conversion (the one exception is Galatians 1:15-16). Rather then setting his experience up as a model of how conversion takes place, Paul emphasizes the grace/favor of God, the reality of the new identity in Christ, and the transformation that is brought about because of faith in Christ.

In his letter to the Colossians he writes: *Thanks to the Father who has qualified us to share in the inheritance of the saints in the kingdom of light. For he has brought us into the kingdom of the Son he loves, in whom we have redemption, the forgiveness of sins* (Colossians 1:12-13). It is interesting to note that in this prayer report Paul identifies himself with the Colossians. What God had done for them he has also done for Paul.

God's call/appointment to Paul to be the Apostle to the Gentiles shaped the rest of his life. This appointment was not something he chose for himself, or somehow had earned -- no, it was thrust upon him. He was *an apostle of Christ Jesus by the will [and command] of God* (1, 2 Corinthians; Eph.; Col. & 1 Tim 1:1 -- "command" 1 Tim. 1:1).

His keen awareness that he had been apprehended by God and thus become a servant of the Lord, meant that he was no longer his own, but had been bought at a price (1 Corinthians 6:19-20). This understanding gave Paul a sense of thankful wonder at God's grace and also placed him under a deep sense of obligation and responsibility as one who must give an account of his service to his Master. Thus he writes:

> *Yet when I preach the gospel, I cannot boast, for I am compelled to preach. Woe is me if I do not preach the gospel! If I preach voluntarily I have a reward; if not voluntarily, I am simply discharging the trust committed to me. (I Corinthians 9:16-17).*

In that statement Paul is echoing what the prophets Jeremiah and Amos wrote:

> *But if I say, 'I will not mention him or speak any more in his name,' his word is in my heart like a burning fire, shut up in*

my bones. I am weary of holding it in; indeed, I cannot (Jeremiah 20:9).

The lion has roared--who will not fear? The Sovereign Lord has spoken-- who can but prophecy? (Amos 3:8).

Paul's call/appointment mirrors that of the prophet Isaiah whose vision of the Lord in the temple, resulted in his conversion-forgiveness, and his call to be a prophet (Is. 6:1-9). Paul also had a vision and received a commission --to be the apostle to the Gentiles (1 Corinthians 15:8-11; Gal. 1:15-16).

Paul regarded his call and apostleship as a favor God bestowed on him…a favor he in no way deserved. He could never forget that he had been a persecutor of the church. He writes:

I became a servant of this gospel by the gift of God's grace given me through the working of his power. Although I am less than the least of all God's people, this grace was given to me: to preach the unsearchable riches of Christ… (Eph. 3:7-8).

For I am least of the apostles and do not even deserve to be called an apostle,because I persecuted the church of God. But by the grace of God I am what I am, and his grace to me was not without effect… (1 Cor. 15:9-10).

I thank Christ Jesus our Lord, who has given me strength, that he considered me faithful, appointing me to his service. Even though I was once a blasphemer and a persecutor and a violent man, I was shown mercy because I acted in ignorance and unbelief. The grace of our Lord was poured out on me abundantly, along with the faith and love that are in Christ Jesus. (1 Timothy 1:12-14)

We often think of Paul as one who was always confident and self assured. However, the apostle also experienced a strong sense of inadequacy. Thus he writes to the Corinthians: *When I came to you,* *brothers, I did not come with eloquence or superior wisdom as I proclaimed to you the testimony about God... I came to you in weakness and fear, and with much trembling. (*1 Corinthians 2:1,3). And when he thought about the effect his presence and preaching had on others, he wrote:

> *For we are to God the aroma of Christ among those who are being saved and those who are perishing. To the one we are the smell of death; to the other, the fragrance of life. And who is equal to such a task?... Not that we are competent to claim anything for ourselves, but our competence comes from God. He has made us competent as ministers of a new covenant--not of the letter but of the Spirit; for the letter kills, but the Spirit gives life. (2 Corinthians 2:15-16, 3:5-6).*

The responsibilities of his calling caused Paul to lean heavily upon God who enabled him to minister, not in his own strength and wisdom, but in the power of the Holy Spirit. One of the lessons that he learned through "the thorn in the flesh" was that his strength and effectiveness lay in his reliance upon Jesus Christ (2 Corinthians 12:7-10). That is the lesson every servant of Christ has had to learn! Zechariah 4:6 *This is the word of the Lord to Zerubbabel: 'Not by might nor by power, but by my Spirit,' says the Lord Almighty.* And Jesus Christ our Lord told his disciples and us, *I am the vine; you are the branches. If a man remains in me and I in him, he will bear much fruit; apart from me you can do nothing* (John 15:5). Paul had learned that *...our competence comes from God. He has made us competent as ministers of a new covenant--not of the letter but of the Spirit...* (2 Corinthians 2:3-6).

It is with a sense of joyful wonder that Paul writes: *I glory in Christ Jesus in my service to God. I will not venture to speak of anything except what God has accomplished through me in leading the Gentiles to obey God by what I have said and done--by the power of signs and miracles, through the power of the Spirit...*(Romans 15:17-19).

The favor of God -- his apostleship-- caused Paul a tremendous amount of suffering --*And of this gospel I was appointed a herald and an apostle and a teacher. That is why I am suffering as I am.* (2 Timothy 1:11-12). Paul gives several lists of what he suffered. As one reads the lists it is difficult not to be overwhelmed by what it cost Paul to be able to say, *I was not disobedient to the vision from heaven* (Acts 26:19), and to affirm at the close of his life, *I have fought the good fight, I have finished the race, I have kept the faith* (2 Timothy 4:7). I would urge you to turn to the end notes and read the lists.[18]

Paul believed in being held accountable

Paul was no lone ranger and thus accountable to no one but himself and God. Quite the contrary--we always find him responsive to authority and being accountable to others. As a persecutor of the church he went to Damascus with the authority of the high priest. After his conversion he connected himself with the Christians in Damascus, went to Arabia for three years and then returned to Damascus (Galatians 1:17). When he went to Jerusalem, *he tried to join the disciples, but they were afraid of him, not believing he really was a disciple. But Barnabas took him and brought him to the apostles...So Saul stayed with them and moved about freely in Jerusalem, speaking boldly in the name of the Lord. He talked and debated with the Grecian Jews, but they tried to kill him. When the brothers learned of this, they took him down to Caesarea and sent him off to Tarsus (Acts 9:26-30).*

Paul, who never seemed to run from a fight or from danger, was willing to submit to the decision of "the brothers"(that is, the leaders in Jerusalem) because of a vision from the Lord (Acts 22:17-21). He was in Tarsus for several years before Barnabas brought him to Antioch where he assisted Barnabas in teaching the new converts. I am convinced that it was in Antioch that Paul learned how to be a missionary to the Gentiles and that his understanding of salvation by grace alone through faith was clarified.

Paul gives us a hint of this when he writes in Galatians 5:11 *Brothers, if I am still preaching circumcision, why am I still being persecuted?* When did Paul ever preach circumcision? The only answer that makes sense to me is in the years he was in Tarsus, before being brought to Antioch. If he preached immediately after his conversion in Damascus and in Jerusalem, I assume he must have continued preaching when he returned to Tarsus. Whereas in Palestine he would speak to Jews, in Tarsus he would have ample opportunity to preach to non-Jews. And what would he, a pharisaic Jewish Christian trained as a rabbi preach?-- Salvation through faith in Jesus and the keeping of law, including circumcision! It would take an indisputable proof by the Holy Spirit to break through Paul's assumptions and training. Antioch, with its Gentile converts who were saved apart from the law or circumcision, was that proof. Since we have no record of a church being founded in Tarsus by Paul, his efforts must have been singularly ineffective. It is not until Antioch, under the guidance of Barnabas, that Paul fully understood *It is by grace you have been saved, through faith -- this not from yourselves, it is a gift of God -- not by works, so no one can boast* (Ephesians 2:8-9).

After his internship in Antioch, Barnabas and Paul were sent out as missionaries by the Holy Spirit, confirmed by the church (Acts 13:2-4). Following their missionary journey they returned to Antioch, the sending church, to report what God had done through them. *They gathered the church together and reported all that God had done through them and how he had opened the door of faith to the Gentiles* (Acts 14:27).

When the gospel preached by Paul and Barnabas and the Church in Antioch was challenged, they agreed to be accountable and to go to Jerusalem *to see the Apostles and elders about this question.*

Some men came down from Judea to Antioch and were teaching the brothers: "Unless you are circumcised, according to the custom taught by Moses, you cannot be saved." This brought Paul and Barnabas into sharp dispute and debate with them. So Paul and Barnabas were appointed, along with some other believers, to go up to Jerusalem to see the apostles and elders about this question (Acts 15:1-2).

What they preached was affirmed by the Council at Jerusalem and they returned to Antioch with a letter and their report. They brought two respected men from Jerusalem to verify what they reported and to encourage the church.

When Paul, accompanied by Silas, [19] are ready to leave on the second missionary journey, again they are sent off by the church (Acts 15:40). They return to Antioch to report what God had done (Acts 18:22). Reporting to the church and being accountable was important to Paul.

When Paul set out on his third missionary journey there is no mention of his being sent out by the church in Antioch, nor does he have a companion from Jerusalem. Perhaps because he was carrying a large amount of money collected for the poor in Jerusalem from the Gentile churches in Greece and the province of Asia and because Antioch had already given a gift (Acts 11:29-30), Paul went directly to Jerusalem at the conclusion of this journey. Because of his arrest, which eventually took him to Rome, Paul was never able to return to his friends in Antioch.

I have given this short account of Paul's life to emphasize that he had a very strong sense of the need to be accountable to others. This recognition that he was accountable was especially strong in his relationship with Christ. He knew that he was not his own, and that he was a servant of Lord. This understanding forms a strong element in his letters.

Part of the motivation which inspired Paul to be faithful in the midst of his suffering and opposition, was that he had a profound awareness that he would give an account of his ministry to Christ. This is a theme which occurs a number of times in his writings.

To the Corinthians he writes, *so then, men ought to regard us as servants of Christ and as those entrusted with the secret things of God. Now it is required that those who have been given a trust must prove faithful.* A few verses later he adds, *He [the Lord] will bring to light what is hidden in darkness and will expose the motives of men's hearts. At that time each will receive his praise from God.* (1 Corinthians 4:1-2, 5).

In 2 Corinthians he writes: *So we make it our goal to please him...for we must all appear before the judgment seat of Christ, that each one may receive what is due him for the things done while in the body, whether good or bad* (2 Corinthians 5:9-10). This subject of the certainty of judgment is also found in Romans 2:16; 14:10-12 and in 2 Timothy 4:1,8. This judgment of which these verses speak is not that which separates mankind from heaven or perdition.

The doctrine of justification by faith, so prominent in Romans and Galatians, refers to the truth that in Christ, God has already declared the verdict on all who have faith in Christ for salvation. Christ Jesus has paid the penalty for our sins (Colossians 2:16-17) and God has given us a righteousness that comes to us by faith in Christ (Philippians 3:7-11). However, there is still the judgment where we will give an account of our faithfulness and will receive our commendation and reward from God (see 1 Corinthians 3:10-15).

This sense of responsibility (*I am obligated both to the Greeks and non-Greeks, both to the wise and the foolish* - Romans 1:14; *For Christ's love compels us, because we are convinced that one died for all and therefore all died* - 2 Corinthians 5:14; *I am compelled to preach. Woe to me if I do not preach the gospel* - 1 Corinthians 9:16) and accountability produced in Paul a holy fear. Thus he writes: *I do all this for the sake of the gospel, that I may share in its blessings...Therefore I do not run like a man running aimlessly; I do not fight like a man beating the air. No I beat my body and make it my slave so that after I have preached to others, I myself will not be disqualified for the prize* (1 Corinthians 9:23, 26-27). Verses 19-22 constitute Paul's philosophy of ministry and gives the rationale for the different shapes that his ministry takes.

Though I am free and belong to no man, I make myself a slave to everyone, to win as many as possible. To the Jews I became as a Jew, to win the Jews. To those under the law (though I myself am not under the law), so as to win those under the law. To the weak I became weak, to win the weak. I have become all things to all men so that by all possible means I might save some. I do all this for the sake of the gospel, that I may share in its blessings. (1 Corinthians 9:19-23).

Summary of Primary Themes

In light of what we have noted about his conversion and call to be an apostle, it may be helpful to summarize what we can confidently conclude were some of the themes that comprised Paul's prayers for himself.

The first aspect is obvious -- praise and thanksgiving. This is such a prominent characteristic of Paul's writings and prayer reports that there is no reason to question that this was a vital part of his personal prayers. As a trained Rabbi, Paul would have used the Psalter in his devotional life. A prominent feature of the Psalms is praise, so it would be natural for this to carry over into Paul's prayer practice as well.

In his letters he breaks out into a doxology again and again. His awareness of the greatness and majesty of God calls forth his adoration. It is a truism that the more one knows and experiences God, the greater is ones sense of wonder and praise.

Paul is thankful for God's mercy, forgiveness, salvation and his calling to be an apostle to the Gentiles. He is grateful for the fact that God has used him to bring salvation to the Gentiles (Romans 15:17-19). It is an amazing aspect of Paul's life, that in spite of his great suffering, he never expresses self-pity, but always expresses a sense of wonder and gratitude.

A second aspect of his personal prayers was his desire to know God the Father and Jesus Christ better. He makes this desire most explicitly in Philippians, which was his last letter written to a church. Although he had been a Christian for at least 30 years and seen the Spirit work mightily in his ministry, he writes:

> *But whatever was for my profit I now consider loss for the sake of Christ. What is more, I consider everything a loss compared to the surpassing greatness of knowing Christ Jesus my Lord, for whose sake I have lost all things. I consider them rubbish, that I may gain Christ and be found in him, not having a righteousness of my own that comes from the law, but that which is through faith in Christ--the righteousness that comes from God and is by faith. I want to know Christ and the power of his resurrection and the fellowship of sharing in his sufferings, becoming like him in his death, and so somehow, to attain to the resurrection from the dead.*
>
> *Not that I have already obtained all this, or have already been made perfect, but I press on to take hold of that for which Christ Jesus took hold of me. Brothers, I do not consider myself yet to have taken hold of it. But one thing I do: Forgetting what is behind and straining toward what is ahead, I press on toward the goal to win the prize for which God has called me heavenward in Christ Jesus. (Philippians 3:7-14)*

This passage unveils Paul's heart and desire more dynamically than any other passage in his writings. And it is interesting to observe that it picks up the themes in his prayer report of Ephesians 1:17-20:

> *I keep asking that the God of our Lord Jesus Christ, the glorious Father, may give you the Spirit of wisdom and revelation, so that you may know him better. I pray also that the eyes of your heart may be enlightened in order that you may know the hope to which he has called you, the riches of his glorious inheritance in the saints, and his incomparably great power for us who believe. That power is like the working of his mighty strength, which he exerted in Christ when he raised him from the dead and seated him at his right hand in the heavenly realms...*

Note that both passages express the desire to know God better, to grasp his intentions for the Christian and to experience the power of God, identified with the power inherent in the resurrection of Jesus. In this light, it is probably not stretching the evidence to say that what he prayed for the churches, also comprised content for his prayers for himself.

One other theme that may have been a part of Paul's prayers for himself was that he might always remain faithful to Christ…no matter the cost. If David could pray: *May those who hope in you not be disgraced because of me, O LORD, the LORD Almighty; may those who seek you not be put to shame because of me* (Psalm 69:6), then it is not unreasonable for Paul to reflect this concern in his own prayers. After all, Paul had such a strong sense of responsibility to Christ and the church that he enjoins them to live lives that are *worthy of their calling, worthy of the Lord, worthy of the kingdom* etc. and several times sets himself as an example to be followed and imitated, [20] that he might well fear that in some way under pressure he might fail. He can write in 2 Timothy 2:10, *Therefore I endure everything for the sake of the elect, that they may obtain the salvation that is in Christ Jesus, with eternal glory.* There are some hints that this was a concern for Paul.

> *I eagerly expect and hope I will in no way be ashamed, but will have sufficient courage so that now as always Christ will be exalted in my body, whether by life or by death. (Philippians 1:20)*

Pray that I may declare it (the gospel) fearlessly, as I should. (Ephesians 6:20)

Pray that I may proclaim it clearly, as I should. (Colossians 4:4)

It is important to observe that each of these requests are found in letters written from prison. There is something about suffering, especially suffering caused by torture, that can erode the spirit and break the will. One may need more than human strength to remain strong and steadfast.

I can imagine the essence of Paul's prayer in this regard to reflect his prayer in 2 Thessalonians 1:11-12. I am taking the liberty to change the pronouns from the second to first person singular in order to make my point.

I constantly pray that our God may count me worthy of his calling, and that by his power he may fulfill every good purpose and every act prompted by my faith. I pray this so that the name of our Lord Jesus may be glorified in me, and I in him, according to the grace of our God and the Lord Jesus Christ.

7. PAUL PRAYED IN TONGUES

In 1 Corinthians 14:18 Paul wrote: *I thank God that I speak in tongues more than all of you. But in church I would rather speak five intelligible words to instruct others than ten thousand words in a tongue.* Paul wrote this in the midst of a discussion of worship and the proper use of the speaking in tongues in a public setting. Although he placed a high value on speaking in a tongue and did not discourage its use in public worship, it seems that he seldom, if ever, spoke in tongues when ministering to the church. In the church setting Paul's emphasis is that everything that is done or said should have value and build up the other worshipers, and speaking in tongues only does this when it is interpreted, which causes it to function much like a prophecy. In private, the gift is a way of praying, praising and communing with God that enriches and edifies the individual. The person's spirit communes with the Spirit of God without the interference and restrictions of the rational mind.

From what Paul wrote in 1 Corinthians 14 we can discern something of what praying in tongues meant to him.

1. The context of 1 Corinthians 14 seems to make it clear that speaking in a tongue is one of the gifts which the Holy Spirit gives.

2. When Paul spoke or prayed in a tongue it was something he chose to do. Speaking in a tongue is not some great emotional or ecstatic experience. The speaker determines if and when they speak in a tongue. They are not so overpowered by the Holy Spirit that they must pray in a tongue. *If anyone speaks in a tongue, two--or at most three--should speak, one at a time, and someone must interpret. If there is no interpreter, the speaker should keep quiet in the church and speak to himself and God... The spirits of the prophets are subject to the control of prophets.* (1 Corinthians 14:27-28, 32). This differentiates the gift of the Spirit from other forms of mantic or ecstatic religious experience.

3. Speaking in a tongue is a prayer language: *For anyone who speaks in a tongue does not speak to men but to God* (v.2). It is also a way of praising God: *If you are praising God with your spirit...you may be giving thanks well enough, but the other man is not edified* (vs. 16-17).

4. Praying in a tongue was one of the ways Paul maintained his amazing spiritual vitality in the face of overwhelming circumstances. He indicates it strengthens and enriches one's own spiritual vitality. *He who speaks in tongue edifies himself* (vs. 4). Although Romans 8:26 has broader application than praying in a tongue, it implies that it may be involved when praying for oneself or someone else.

5. For one with the intellect and training of Paul to rejoice that he speaks in tongues is somewhat surprising, *For if I pray in a tongue, my spirit prays but my mind is unfruitful* (vs. 14). *For anyone who speaks in a tongue...utters mysteries with his spirit* (vs. 2).

It is a well known fact that the creative powers of a person function best when the rational thinking is disengaged. One of the things that makes it hard for us to hear God is our reliance on our rational faculties. But as God says through Isaiah the prophet: '*For my thoughts are not your thoughts, neither are your ways my ways,' declares the LORD* (Isaiah 55:8). Paul's education and rabbinical training would be a major barrier to his ability to receive revelation from God, for he would always tend to think in patterns and categories that were familiar and comfortable for him. If, however, the revelation was given to Paul in a non-rational way, the usual rational barriers would be removed and the revelation would be received complete, not piecemeal or in a manner that would make one struggle in order to comprehend and assimilate it. The revelation would be received first in one's spirit and then through the gift of interpretation, into the rational mind. This is why Paul urges the Corinthians *For anyone who speaks in a tongue...utters mysteries with his spirit* (vs.2)...*For this reason anyone who speaks in a tongue should pray that he may interpret what he says* (vs. 13).

The word translated "mysteries" may be a clue to corroborate what we have just said. The word is generally used with words which indicate something revealed or proclaimed. It thus becomes almost a technical term meaning that something that was not known or was hidden in the past has now been made known and has become "something dynamic and compelling."[21] In Colossians 1:18-29 Paul makes it clear that the mystery is Christ and the redemption God provided through him for all people -- both Jews and non-Jews.

The mystery has become the very essence of the understanding and presentation of the Gospel. Romans 16:25-26 provides us with the basic understanding of "mystery" in Paul's writings:

> *Now to him who is able to establish you by my gospel and the proclamation of Jesus Christ, according to the revelation of the mystery hidden for long ages past, but now revealed and made known through the prophetic writings by the command of the eternal God, so that all nations might believe and obey him...*

Although speaking in a tongue would generally be an aspect of private prayer and praise, on occasion it could become a vehicle for God revealing deeper things relating to the meaning of the life, ministry, death and resurrection of Jesus Christ. It could be one of the ways that the promise of Jesus regarding the ministry of the Holy Spirit would be fulfilled:

But when he, the Spirit of truth, comes, he will guide you into all truth. He will not speak on his own; he will speak only what he hears, and he will tell you what is to come (John 16:13).

Paul picks up this theme in 1 Corinthians 2:11b-13.

No one knows the thoughts of God except the Spirit of God. We have not received the spirit of the world but the Spirit of God, that we may understand what God has freely given us. This is what we speak, not in words taught us by human wisdom but in words taught by the Spirit, expressing spiritual truths in spiritual words.

For the Apostle Paul, then, speaking in a tongue was a very practical way of building up his spiritual life by enabling him to commune with God spirit to Spirit and receive the special revelations which he needed in order to fulfill his role of apostle-teacher.

8. PAUL LIVED IN THE PRESENCE OF GOD

People who insist on being pious are not much fun to be around. There is an old story of two Puritans who were walking through a field resplendent with wild flowers. One said to the other, “Isn’t this beautiful?” To which the other Puritan replied, “I am glad that I have come to the place in my spiritual life when there is nothing beautiful in this wicked world!” Religious people often have a difficult time just having fun and enjoying life to the full. Yet Jesus said that he had come to give us life abundant (John 10:10). We know that Jesus was a fun guy to be around because sinners, tax collectors, and the common people enjoyed his company, and such people do not enjoy being around a kill joy. It was the religious people, the pious Pharisees who had trouble with Jesus.

One of the remarkable things about the Apostle Paul was his ability to make and keep deep friendships. One needs only to read his letters to observe the large number of people he mentions by name. He obviously had one of those dominating personalities that caused others to look to him for leadership. Luke emphasizes this in Acts 27, when he describes Paul, the prisoner headed for Rome and under guard, who nevertheless is the one who takes charge as the ship is in a great storm and about to be wrecked. From Luke's account it is obvious that Paul has even won the friendship of the centurion and the captain of the ship. Paul was not a "pious" person in the negative sense of that word. He must have been a very interesting and delightful personality. Yet he instructs the Thessalonian Christians to "pray constantly", or to "pray without ceasing."

When one reads some of the literature on prayer, especially from a monastic perspective, the only way to pray without ceasing is to live a solitary life dedicated to prayer, fasting, and contemplation. Paul knows nothing of this kind of life. He always has people around him. He is always interacting, witnessing, preaching, healing. When he is alone, as he was in Athens, he was miserable. So for Paul, to pray without ceasing did not mean to withdraw from people or from the normal demands of life.

The instructions of the Apostle: "Be joyful always; pray continually; give thanks in all circumstances, for this is God's will for you in Christ Jesus" (1 Thessalonians 5:16-18), means very simply that we are to live in the presence of God so that "whatever you do, whether in word or deed, do it all in the name of the Lord Jesus, giving thanks to God the Father through him" (Colossians 3:17 & elsewhere). In fact, Colossians 3:12-17 is a good example of what it means to live in the presence of God. To live in God's presence is not some "other worldly" experience. Just note the aspects Paul mentions which really relate to what it means to live continuously in God‘s presence:

Colossians 3:12-17 -- To live in God's presence means:

1. To know who you are -- you are chosen, holy, and deeply loved.
2. You consciously chose to display compassion, kindness, humility, gentleness, and patience. And you put up with others, forgiving wrongs and showing the same love for others as Christ has shown

to you. This love brings harmony and makes our relationships dance with its music.

3. You let the peace, the wholeness of Christ, rule in your heart and in your relationships.

4. You are grateful.

5. You allow the word of Christ to enrich your life and humbly and joyfully teach and learn from others.

6. So whatever you do you do it all in the name of the Lord Jesus, giving thanks to God the Father through him.

To live in God's presence, to pray constantly,[22] is profoundly practical and simply means that our lives, as well as our minds and mouths, are a prayer of joyful, thankful, submission to God and an expression of our desire to honor, please and serve him in all we do or say.

PRAYER PRINCIPLE #6

We need to learn to live in the presence of God.

Being a follower of Jesus is not a part time endeavor. We must learn to live each day in God's presence.

Proverbs 4:23 tells us:

Above all things, keep your heart with all vigilance, for out of it are the issues of life. **What does it mean to you to keep your heart? What do you do to keep your heart?**

Colossians 3:12-17 is a combination of things that are personal and things that involve our relationship with others. In what ways do other people affect your relationship with God? How do you forgive when you do not want to forgive? What is forgiveness?

PART TWO

PAUL'S TEACHING ABOUT PRAYER

Part 1: THE HOLY SPIRIT AND PRAYER[23]

Paul's greatest contribution to our understanding of prayer is his teaching about the role of the Holy Spirit in prayer.

If it were not for the temptation accounts of Jesus, which are part of his private teaching to the disciples and not part of his public teaching, and the garden scene in Genesis 3, we would not understand that in temptation we are not battling only our lower nature, but that we are being attacked by Satan. If all we had was the insightful description of temptation in James 1:13-15, which does not mention Satan but only one's own evil desires, we would never suspect that there was an outside foe who uses our natural weaknesses to entice us away from our obedience and dependence on God. But because of Jesus, and the temptation of Eve, we know that there are three persons involved in temptation: ourselves, Satan, and God. And thus we also know that in temptation Satan uses that which is natural and good to cause us to abandon our dependence upon God.

So also in prayer, we would not really know that we are being helped by God's Spirit were it not for the instruction given by the Apostle Paul. In fact, Paul's great contribution to the subject of prayer is his teaching about the Holy Spirit's role in prayer. No other Biblical writer connects prayer and the Holy Spirit.[24]

The key passages relating to prayer and the Spirit are:

- Romans 8:12-27
- Romans 8:12-17 tell us of the witness of the Spirit
- Romans 8:26-27 tell us of the intercession of the Spirit
- Galatians 4:6 tells us of the witness of the Spirit (=Rom. 8:15)
- Ephesians 5:18 (and also Jude 20) tells us to "pray in the Spirit."

These are the only verses in the Bible that speak of the role of the Holy Spirit in prayer.

The most important of Paul's instructions regarding the Holy Spirit and prayer is Romans 8:26-27 -- *In the same way, the Spirit helps us in our weakness. We do not know what we ought to pray, but the Spirit himself intercedes for us with groans that words cannot express. And he who searches our hearts knows the mind of the Spirit, because the Spirit intercedes for the saints in accordance with God's will.*

If the Apostle Paul had not written these words, we would not understand that prayer is not simply our expressing our desires and needs to God. In a deep and profound way, God, through the Holy Spirit is involved, not only in hearing our prayers but also in the very act of prayer itself.

There are several observations which need to be made:

1. We have Two Intercessors

In Romans 8 we are informed that we have two persons who are interceding for us. In verses 26-27 we are told that the Spirit intercedes for us, and then in verse 35 we are informed that Christ also intercedes for us: *Who is he that condemns? Christ Jesus, who died--more than that, who was raised to life--is at the right hand of God and is also interceding for us.*

It is encouraging to understand that we have two intercessors: Christ and the Holy Spirit. However, we need to also understand that their intercession is not the same. They are different in at least two ways:

1. Their location different: Christ is in heaven, at the right hand of God and the Spirit is here on earth, dwelling in the believer.

2. Their intercession is different: There is nothing we can do to either

assist or hinder Christ's intercession for us. His intercession is objective, it is "for us." On the other hand, the Spirit's intercession is dependent upon our cooperation. He *helps us in our weakness. We do not know what we ought to pray, but the Spirit himself intercedes for us with groans that words cannot express.* If we do not pray, the Spirit does not intercede.

This cooperation between us and the Spirit is essential for us to understand if we are to begin to grasp the role and power of the Spirit in our lives. It is emphasized also in Romans 8:15-16: *...but you received the Spirit of sonship* (literally, *adoption). And by him (the Spirit) we cry, "Abba, Father." The Spirit himself testifies with our spirit that we are God's children.* We do the crying but the Spirit enables us. We testify that we are God's child, and the Spirit testifies "with our spirit", that is, he confirms and assures. Notice that the Spirit both enables the cry of our deep awareness of God as our Father, and he testifies, not simply to our spirit, but with our spirit. As we affirm our new status with the Father, the Spirit affirms our conviction. In John 15:26-27, Jesus tells the disciples that *the Spirit will testify about me, and you also must testify about me...* The relationship of the believer with the Spirit is one of cooperation in which our act is assisted by the Spirit and brought to fruition through the Spirit.

2. The Spirit helps us

The word translated "help"[25] is an interesting word which also draws a picture of this cooperation between us and the Spirit. The word is difficult to translate into English, because it is a word which has two prefixes: it is the word *sun-anti-lombonomai* (I have separated the prefixes for illustration). The basic word means "to grasp, to take hold of." The prefix *sun* means "together with" and thus the word means "to grasp together with", or to help. The prefix *anti* means "instead of, or in opposition to." This seems almost contradictory, "take hold together with, instead of," but it illustrates a wonderful truth: The Holy Spirit assists us, he "takes hold together with us", but when we come to the end of our abilities, he "holds on instead of us," and does what we cannot do for ourselves--in this case, interceding for us with groans that words cannot express.

3. The Spirit helps us in our weakness

It is important to observe that *the Spirit helps us in our weakness.* This introduces us to a topic that is key, both to the theology of the Apostle Paul and to our understanding of our own situation. We are WEAK, even though we may think we are strong.[26] Although the reference here is to prayer, it would be a mistake to restrict the weakness to our not knowing what we should pray. That is only one small aspect of our weakness which characterizes our life situation.

We need to grasp the reality of the tension in which we as Christians live our lives and that contributes to our weakness. There are at least three aspects of this tension which we must consider.

A. The "already-not yet' aspect of salvation

Although we are redeemed now -- present reality; we still await the full reality of our redemption -- future expectation. Paul writes, *we ourselves, who have the firstfruits of the Spirit, groan inwardly as we wait eagerly for our adoption as sons, the redemption of our bodies* (Ro. 8:23). And again, *our salvation is nearer now than when we first believed* (Ro. 13:11).

Although we have received the Spirit, it is only the firstfruits of the Spirit, or the down payment on our inheritance (Eph. 1:14) which we have received. The full payment and inheritance is still future.

Although we are God's children now and have been forgiven and received the Spirit; nevertheless, we must still struggle with the natural self that is still tainted with the effects of the rebellion (the fall). We are still in the flesh and there is a war between flesh and Spirit. Paul spells this out in some detail in Galatians 5:17: *The sinful nature desires what is contrary to the Spirit, and the Spirit what is contrary to the sinful nature. They are in conflict with each other, so that you do not do what your want.*

The word translated *sinful nature* in the NIV translation is the word that literally means "flesh". But as Paul uses the word it often does not refer simply to our fleshly bodies but means the natural self apart from God. This "flesh," in and of itself, is not inherently sinful, for it is through our bodies and personalities and natural abilities that we serve God, and it is through our bodies and personalities and natural abilities that we disobey God. I agree with Oswald Chambers when he wrote: "Human nature is earthly, it is sordid, but it is not bad, the thing that makes it bad is sin."[27] Christ took on our humanity, and lived in the flesh and thus showed us that it is possible to please God through the natural gifts of bodily, fleshly life. The goal of the disciples of Jesus is to so consecrate our fleshly life[28] that it is wholly consecrated and abandoned to God so that it becomes the vehicle and instrument through which His will is done in and by us. The Christian life is not so much a commitment as it is a surrender to God. The concept of commitment emphasizes our will, effort, and strength, while the concept of surrender stresses the release of our lives -- body, soul, and spirit -- to Christ. This abandonment to Christ does not diminish our selfhood, but rather releases and enhances all of our energies so that we can become truly an instrument of God. This giving up of our control enables us to learn to live under the new management of the Holy Spirit.

B. We are a bundle of contradictions and must learn to live under the new management of the Spirit

We love God but find ourselves at times being disobedient. We are committed disciples of Christ, yet yield to the temptations of the flesh. We are humble servants of Christ, but continue to be self-centered, selfish, want to be in control, and act as though we are independent of his rule. We are saved but continue to allow sin to mar our walk with Christ. We are God's children but far from living in perfect fellowship with him.

Many Christians live with guilt, self-condemnation, and doubt. Sometimes we may even say to ourselves, "What right do I have to claim to be a Christian? Christians shouldn't have the thoughts I have." "If I have the Holy Spirit, why do I have to work so hard to be obedient and live in fellowship with Christ?" In our attempt to live the Christian life we may adopt a perfectionist mentality and hedge our lives around with a multitude of rules and regulations, all designed to keep us from sinning or wandering away from our commitment to Christ -- yet each of these hedges adds to our guilt when we fail. We believe that sin should have no place in our lives, and that if only we walked close enough to God we would not have to struggle the way we do. But this is a false expectation and indicates that we still do not understand the reality of our life-situation, which is weakness.

One of the realities of the Christian life is that we live in the tension of "already-not yet". We are both spiritual and fleshly, holy and profane. This tension is something that we never completely escape because it is rooted in the reality of the freedom which is ours in Christ Jesus -- *If the Son sets you free, you will be free indeed* (John 8:36). The freedom which sin gives is illusionary for the more one practices sin, the less free one is to not to continue to sin. Sin becomes a habit which destroys our freedom not to do that which is sinful. But the freedom Christ gives is real, for he never removes our ability to disobey him. Someone has written, "Every good and perfect thing stands moment by moment on the razors edge and must be fought for." Bad habits enslave us and are hard to break, but right behavior never enslaves us, it is easy to slip back into our self-centered control and to do that which in our better moments we do not want to do. Every day, again and again, we are forced to consciously choose God's way. This is not as easy as it sounds. C. S. Lovett, insightfully notes that if you want to know how Satan will tempt you today, just look in the mirror. Temptation always comes in terms of our own best self interest![29] We need the Spirit's help if we are truly to discern the schemes of the evil one and choose what is the good and acceptable and perfect will of God (Romans 12:2).

The way of sin is irrational, for it often causes us to do the very things that destroy what we really want. Oswald Chambers makes an insightful observation when he wrote:

"We take a rational view of life and say that a man by controlling his instincts and by educating himself, can produce a life which will slowly evolve into the life of God. But as we go on, we find the presence of something which we have not taken into consideration, viz., sin, and it upsets all our calculations. Sin has made the basis of things wild and not rational. We have to recognize that sin is a fact, not a defect; sin is red-handed mutiny against God. Either God or sin must die in my life. The New Testament brings us right down to this one issue. If sin rules in me, God's life in me will be killed; if God rules in me, sin in me will be killed. There is no possible ultimate but that."[30]

Part of our problem is that we must learn to live under the new management of the Spirit of God. We continually fall back on the protective and comfortable reliance on ourselves and think that we can do it and only need God's help in the difficult or unusual circumstances. But the Christian life is not one of intermittent reliance on God, but rather one of learning to live constantly in his presence. Proverbs 3:5-6 says it well: *Trust in the Lord with all your heart, and lean not on your own understanding; in all you ways acknowledge him, and he will direct your paths (KJ).*[31] While this is our goal we must not forget that we are engaged in a struggle.

Paul after describing the inward battle which the Christian experiences, with its contradictions, cries out, *What a wretched man I am! Who will deliver me from this body of death? Thanks be to God--through Jesus Christ our Lord!* But he does not stop there with this cry of victory but goes on to say, *So then, I myself in my mind am a slave to God's law, but in the sinful nature (literally "the flesh") a slave to the law of sin.* (Romans 7:25).

We are uncomfortable with the end of verse 25, and in fact with the whole section of Romans 7:14-25. It does not fit with our triumphant and victorious view of what the Christian life should be. Many scholars regard it as a parenthetical section which describes Paul's pre-Christian life, and that it is an interruption to his argument explaining salvation in Romans 5-8. However, today more and more scholars view it as a vital part of the argument which stresses the already-not yet tension under which we live as citizens of two worlds.[32] In Romans 6, the theme is that we are set free from the dominion of sin, in Romans 7 the subject is that we are set free from the dominion of the law. Our salvation rests, not in our self efforts but in Jesus Christ. Romans 8 has the theme of life in the Spirit. As Paul states in Romans 8:1-4:

> *Therefore, there is no condemnation for those who are in Christ Jesus, because through Christ Jesus the law of the Spirit of life set me free from the law of sin and death. For what the law could not do in that it was weakened by the sinful nature (literally, the flesh), God did by sending his own Son in*

the likeness of sinful man to be a sin offering. And so he condemned sin in sinful man (literally, the flesh), in order that the righteous requirements of the law might be fully met in us, who do not live according to the sinful nature (literally, the flesh) but according to the Spirit.

Although we are now saved, forgiven, and adopted (Ro. 8:15) into God's family through Jesus Christ, in Romans 8:22-23 Paul describes the tension of the "not yet:" *We know that the whole creation has been groaning as in the pains of childbirth right up to the present time. Not only so, but we ourselves, who have the first fruits of the Spirit groan inwardly as we wait eagerly for our adoption as sons, the redemption of our bodies.*

In his book Glad Hearts *The Joys of Believing and Challenges of Belonging*, James Hawkinson recounts that "Covenanter Lloyd Ahlem once said in my hearing that the most difficult challenge every individual faces in this life is to move his or her ego from the center of their consciousness and allow God his rightful place in that center. But that is easier said than done, as we all know. Our egos fight hard for prominence and place."[33]

I rejoice that *there is no condemnation for those who are in Christ Jesus, because through Christ Jesus the law of the Spirit of life set me free from the law of sin and death* (Romans 8:1). The law of the Spirit of life is salvation by grace energized by the Spirit. The law of sin and death is the notion, inspired by the evil one, that I can somehow by my own effort break the hold of sin on my life and earn and deserve a place in heaven. H. Orton Wiley made a comment in a class lecture that has helped to set me free from my sense of failure to be the disciple I wanted to be. He said, "It is not our sin that separates us from God, but rather our rejection of Jesus Christ, who is God's remedy for our sin, that separates us from God." In a sermon Wesley Nelson, former professor of homiletics at North Park Theological Seminary, observed: "The power of sin is not its power to make us disobey God. The power of sin is its power to make us happy in our sins." I am so glad that the Holy Spirit helps us in our weakness by convicting of sin, calling us to repentance, and applying the redemption that is ours in Christ to our hearts.

I resonate to the suggestion of Paul Billheimer that prayer and our learning to use the spiritual resources which God has made available for us when dealing with temptation, the onslaught of evil, our struggle with full obedience, the reliance on the Holy Spirit, etc. are "on-the-job" training experiences which are preparing us for the work God has for us to do in eternity.[34]

This struggle we are in is designed, not to destroy us, but to bring to reality the fullness of God's redemptive power and grace in our lives. Henri Nouwen has observed that all true ministry emerges out of our own woundedness, just as our redemption emerges from the woundedness of our Lord Jesus Christ.[35] We want to serve God out of our strength and forget that *God chose the foolish things of the world to shame the wise; God chose the weak things of the world to shame the strong. He chose the lowly things of this world and the despised things--and the things that are not--to nullify the things that are, so that no one may boast before him* (1 Corinthians 1:27-29).

C. We are citizens of two worlds

The battle in which we are engaged is, at least in part, because we are citizens of two "worlds". "*Our citizenship is in heaven*" (Phil. 3:20), but we still live on the earth in the flesh and look forward to the coming of Christ *"who will change our lowly bodies to be like his glorious body."* This dual citizenship causes a problem: We are no longer simply fleshly and we are not yet fully spiritual. Thus the Apostle tells us in Galatians 5:17, *The sinful nature (literally, the flesh) desires what is contrary to the Spirit, and the Spirit what is contrary to the sinful nature. They are in conflict with each other, so that you do not do what you want.* He then adds: *But if you are led by the Spirit, you are not under law,* i.e., our failure to live the perfectly obedient life does not bring condemnation because we are saved by grace and not by our own self-achievement. As Zechariah 4:6 states: *It* is *not by might nor by power, but by my Spirit, says the Lord Almighty.*

It is not by accident that Paul then goes on in Galatians 5 to describe the *acts of the sinful nature (the flesh)* and then contrasts this with *the fruit of the Spirit...against [which] there is no law.* The acts of the flesh are the result of our living for ourselves and apart from God; the fruit of the Spirit, on the other hand, are the natural result of living by the Spirit (Gal. 5:25). The fruit are not the result of our self-achievement but rather of the action of the Spirit of God in our lives. As Jesus observed: *A good tree brings forth good fruit.* Whether a person is spiritually alive and healthy is proved, not by their words but, by their behavior. To live according to the flesh has its consequences and living by the Spirit of God has its fruit.

There is an old Swedish hymn by Lina Sandell which the immigrants loved to sing and which asks a pertinent question:

> *"Pray that Jesus may awaken Spirit-life forever new.*
> *Pray that sin may be forsaken which breeds only death in you!*
> *Ask yourself each day he gives,*
> *'Do I live?'"*[36]

Jesus told the parable of the seed growing by itself in Mark 4:26-29: *This is what the kingdom of God is like. A man scatters seed on the ground. Night and day, whether he sleeps or gets up, the seed sprouts and grows though he does not know how. All by itself the soil produces grain--first the stalk, then the head, then the full kernel in the head. As soon as the grain is ripe, he puts the sickle to it, because the harvest has come.* The farmer does not cause the seed to grow--*the seed sprouts and grows though he does not know how. All by itself the soil produces grain.* There are, however, some things which the farmer does--he prepares the soil and scatters the seed and then harvests the grain when it is ripe. Without the farmer's actions there is no harvest.

There is a natural development in the life of one who is seeking to "keep in step with the Spirit." We do not cause healthy spiritual growth, that is the Spirit's work, but we can do the things that make this growth possible. Some of the things we can do is to live constantly in the forgiveness and grace of our Lord Jesus Christ, remain sensitive to the corrections and nudging of the Holy Spirit, read and study the Scripture (2 Timothy 2:15), pray with praise, thanksgiving and intercession, worship regularly with God's people, obey God, and when we have failed, confess our sin and accept God's cleansing, and constantly acknowledge our need of the Spirit's help. We must rely on the Spirit convicting us of sin because as the hymn writer puts it, we are "prone to wander, Lord I feel it; prone to leave the God I love."[37]

When we understand how weak we are and how difficult it is for us to keep our hearts and minds centered on Christ Jesus, then we will also discover why we must lean so hard on God's Spirit and how wonderful it is that "the Spirit helps us in our weakness." C. O. Rosenius observes

"When conversion occurs a person experiences the new birth of the Spirit (see 2 Corinthians 5:17). But Paul implies that it is also a continuing and progressive transformation 'by the renewal' of one's mind. One is not to be satisfied with the spiritual mentality that was present at conversion, but there must be progression and growth. This is essential not only for strength to overcome temptations triumphantly, but in order that service may be rendered circumspectly for the what is good and acceptable and perfect' (Romans 12:2). Only the mind of a person who is in Christ is qualified to 'prove' and differentiate or examine what is God's will…It appears that what Paul desired to convey is that the more we become changed by the renewal of our minds in Christ, the more we will 'make it our aim to please him' (2 Corinthians 5:9)."[38]

Spiritual growth and the display of the fruit of the Spirit is a natural result of a healthy spiritual life which enables one to 'keep in step with the Spirit." The Spirit is the "Spirit of life in Christ Jesus" (Romans 8:1) who also "gives life (energy, health, vitality) to our mortal bodies" (Romans 8:11). Although this last reference is generally understood to refer to the hope of the future resurrection,[39] I believe that is too narrow an interpretation because everything that Paul mentions in Romans 8:1-11 has reference to the present life of the believer, rather than to the future consummation of our hope. It is precisely because we are frail, weak, struggling people that we need the assistance of the Holy Spirit who "gives life to our mortal bodies" and breaks our bondage to the dominion of sin. As Charles Wesley wrote in his famous hymn, *O for a Thousand Tongues:* "He breaks the power of cancelled sin, he sets the prisoner free…"

4. One Challenge of Prayer

We do not know what we ought to pray

It does not make much difference whether we translate this *We do not know how to pray as we ought* or as the NIV has translated. The fact of the matter is that we only see things from our perspective. God's concern is not to answer our prayers as we imagine they should be answered. God's concern is to form us into the likeness of Christ. There is an insightful meditation in *Streams in the Desert* that speaks to this point.

"Often it is simply the answers to our prayers that cause many of the difficulties in the Christian life. We pray for patience, and our Father sends demanding people our way who test us to the limit, 'because…*suffering produces perseverance'* (Rom. 5:3). We pray for a submissive spirit, and God sends suffering again, for we learn to be obedient in the same way Christ '*learned obedience from what he suffered"* (Heb. 5:8).

We pray to be unselfish, and God gives us opportunities to sacrifice by placing other people's needs first and by laying down our lives for other believers. We pray for strength and humility, and 'a messenger of Satan' (2 Cor. 12:7) comes to torment us until we lie on the ground pleading for it to be withdrawn.

We pray to the Lord, as His apostles did, saying, 'Increase our faith!' (Luke 17:5). Then our money seems to take wings and fly away; our children become critically ill;. . . or some other new trial comes upon us, requiring more faith than we have ever before experienced.

We pray for a Christlike life that exhibit's the humility of a lamb. Then we are asked to perform some lowly task, or we are unjustly accused and given no opportunity to explain; for 'he was led like a lamb to the slaughter, and…did not open he mouth' (Is. 53:7).

We pray for gentleness and quickly face a storm of temptation to be harsh and irritable. We pray for quietness, and suddenly every nerve is stressed to its limit with tremendous tension so that we may learn that when He sends His peace, no one can disturb it.

We pray for love for others, and God sends unique suffering by sending people our way who are difficult to love and who say things that get on our nerves and tear at our heart. He does this because 'love is patient, love is kind. . .It is not rude,. it is not easily angered. . . *.It always protects,* always trusts, always hopes, always perseveres. Love never fails.' (1 Cor. 13:4-5, 7-8).

Yes, we pray to be like Jesus, and God's answer is: 'I have tested you in the furnace of affliction' (Isa. 48:10); 'Will your courage endure or your hands be strong?' (Ezek. 2:6); 'Can you drink the cup?' (Matt. 20:33).

The way to peace and victory is to accept every circumstance and every trial as being straight from the hand of our loving Father; to live 'with him in the heavenly realms' (Eph. 2:6), above the clouds, in the very presence of His throne; and to look down from glory on our circumstances as being lovingly and divinely appointed.[40]

In addition when we pray for others, there is the added complexity of their lives, desires, and what God is doing to bring them to conformity to Christ. How wonderful it is to understand that *the Spirit helps us in our weakness...and intercedes for us.*

5. The Spirit Intercedes for us

> *The Spirit helps us in our weakness. We do not know what we ought to pray, but the Spirit himself intercedes for us with groans that words cannot express.*

To intercede means to speak or plead for another. The Spirit takes our prayers and pleads on our behalf to the Father. A number of scholars regard this "groans that words cannot express" as referring to speaking in tongues. But if that is so, it implies that the Spirit only intercedes for those who have this spiritual gift--and this leaves out a vast number of Christians and even our Lord Jesus, who as far as we know, never spoke in tongues.

Since Paul has not referred to spiritual gifts yet in this letter to the Romans, and when he does so in chapter 12, he fails to mention the gift of speaking in tongues, we need to consider a more natural meaning of this phrase. In the preceding verses Paul has used the word "groan" twice. Once of creation and once of the believer (Romans 8:22, 23). There the word is expressive of the deep longing for the fulfillment of redemption...*the redemption of our bodies... For in this hope we were saved* (v. 24). This is the hope of the kingdom of God in which God's will is done on earth as it is in heaven (Matthew 6:10). So when Christians pray with regard to illness, sin, injustice, the conversion of others, the problems of life, etc., they are ultimately praying for God to manifest his rule so that the forces of evil are vanquished. Because of our weakness as humans we often express this poorly. The Spirit takes our concerns and interprets it to the Father.

One of the things this verse teaches us is that true prayer is not a simple matter of verbal fluency, but rather of the intent and burden of the heart. This is good news, for God looks at the heart and the Spirit interprets our deep desires that arise out of love and faith and a desire for God's perfect will to be done. *The Spirit helps us in our weakness* and *intercedes for us with groans that words cannot express.*

6. We are to Pray in the Spirit

In Ephesians 6:18 we are instructed to *pray in the Spirit on all occasions with all kinds of prayers and requests.* What does it mean to "pray in the Spirit?" We need to be very careful that we do not equate this with speaking in tongues, though "with all kinds of prayers" certainly would include praying in tongues. The only place in which Paul speaks of praying in tongues is 1 Corinthians 14:14-15 -- *For if I pray in a tongue, my spirit prays, but my mind is unfruitful. So what shall I do? I will pray with my spirit, but I will also pray with my mind; I will sing with my spirit, but I will also sing with my mind.*

Notice that the word "spirit" refers not to the Holy Spirit but to the human spirit. When a person prays using the spiritual gift of speaking in tongues, s/he is praying with their spirits rather than with their mind. Paul tells us that this edifies the person who prays. Arthur Wallis in his insightful book, *Pray in the Spirit: The Work of the Holy Spirit in the Ministry of Prayer,* writes:

"It is clear, then, that in 1 Corinthians 14 praying with the spirit is equivalent to praying with the spiritual gift. This involves the human spirit as distinct from the human mind. The emphasis here is not on the Holy Spirit, as with the expression 'in the Spirit', though of course His presence and activity are implied, for we cannot pray rightly with the spirit, or even with the mind for that matter, apart from the Holy Spirit. But it is important to see where the emphasis lies.

"Let us take this comparison further: Paul says, 'I will pray with the spirit and I will pray with the mind also.' The repetition, 'I will pray …

and I will pray …' proves that Paul envisages two kinds of praying, not as some have supposed, the human spirit and the human mind praying together. He means that he will pray with his new tongue (Mk. 16:17) and he will pray with his native tongue. But in Ephesians 6:18 he exhorts us 'Pray *at all times* in the Spirit.' So praying is only sometimes 'with the spirit' (i.e. in tongues) but 'at all times in the Spirit.'

"Paul contrasts 'in the Spirit' with 'in the flesh' (Rom. 8:9). So the alternative to 'praying in the Spirit' is praying in the flesh. No wonder he says 'Pray *at all times* in the Spirit.' But in 1 Corinthians 14 the contrast is between praying 'with the spirit' and praying 'with the mind', both of which may be 'in the Spirit' and pleasing to God. 'In the Spirit' is therefore a much broader concept than 'with the spirit.' To identify the one with the other is to imply that all the great intercessors of the Old Testament and even our blessed Lord Himself did not pray in the Spirit because, to our knowledge, they did not pray in tongues.

"Now prayer is not the only activity 'in the Spirit' requires of us. The New Testament speaks of living in the Spirit, walking in the Spirit, worshipping in the Spirit, joying in the Spirit, etc. All that is meant is that each activity is performed by the power and enabling of the Holy Spirit. This is in exact agreement with what we have already learned is meant by praying in the Spirit. Expressed in the most practical terms it means that the Holy Spirit inspires, guides, energizes, and sustains the praying."[41]

Wallis believes the context of the two times we are told to pray in the Spirit (Ephesians 6:18 and Jude 20) is instructive. The reference in Ephesians concludes the listing of the armor of God in the believer's warfare and the Jude reference follows the injunction to build ourselves up in our most holy faith. "So it is in the context of battling and building that we are exhorted to 'pray in the Spirit'. These two figures in fact sum up what the Christian life is all about. We are reminded of Nehemiah and his compatriots engaged in their God given task of restoring Jerusalem, sword in one hand and trowel in the other… If we are to build a successful conclusion and to wage a victorious warfare against our implacable foe we must learn to pray in the Spirit."[42]

7. There is another facet to praying "in the Spirit."

James Torrence, in a lecture, "The place of Jesus Christ in Worship,"[43] which I heard him give, stated that the only true and perfect worshipper is Jesus Christ and by means of the Holy Spirit we are enabled to participate in Jesus' perfect worship and prayer to the Father. Through the Spirit we are also enabled to participate in Christ's redemptive ministry to the world. This lecture impacted me greatly because it meant that the ministry was not my ministry but Christ's, and that my prayers are not simply the expression of my desires, but are interpreted so that they are in accord with God's will. It meant that I was not in this battle alone, but that if I would keep in step with the Spirit, I would become an instrument of God's grace and love.

As we live in the Spirit and pray in the Spirit, we are given the privilege of participating in Christ's ministry to the Father (praise and glorifying) and to the world (compassion, proclamation and evangelism). Jesus sent *the gift my Father promised* (Acts 1:4), who is *the Spirit of adoption* (Romans 8:15), who affirms to us our new status as children of God and who is also *The Spirit of life in Christ Jesus,* and who sets us free from the law (dominion) of sin and death (Romans 8:1-2), and *who helps us in our weakness* and intercedes for us according to the will of God (Romans 8:26-27). As we learn to live in the Spirit we will also discover a new joy in Jesus Christ our Lord. Our focus will not be on the Spirit but upon our Lord Jesus. As Jesus said about the Spirit: *He will glorify me* (John 16:14 K.J.).

PRAYER PRINCIPLE #7

The Holy Spirit intercedes for us.

How has your understanding and experience of the Holy Spirit been enriched in the last three months?

In what ways has the Holy Spirit helped you recently?

Knowing that the Holy Spirit intercedes for us influences our prayer life. In what ways has this understanding informed you personal journey of learning to live under new management?

PART II: PAUL'S TEACHING ABOUT PRAYER

Although Paul's greatest contribution to our understanding of prayer is his teaching on the role of the Holy Spirit in prayer, scattered through his letters are a number of instructions that also enrich our practice of prayer. Most of Paul's teaching on prayer is occasional in nature, by which I mean that the instructions come out of the context of what he is writing, rather than an intentional focus on the subject of prayer. For the sake of catching the impact of what he says, I have divided his teaching according to the major thrust that he makes.

THE ROLE OF JESUS CHRIST IN PRAYER

It is not surprising that Christian prayer should have its center in Jesus Christ. The Christ event has changed everything, and neither Paul nor any other writer of the New Testament ever presents any kind of apologetic argument as to why an orthodox Jew trained as a rabbi would now make his prayers with reference to Jesus. There are two great truths which Paul teaches with regard to Christ and prayer that supports what is said elsewhere in the New Testament and impact greatly our practice.

1. We come to the Father through Jesus Christ

In the rich passage of Ephesians 2:11-22, Paul writes about the amazing work which Jesus Christ accomplished. He states this more succinctly in Colossians 1:13-14, *for he [God] has rescued us from the dominion of darkness and brought us into the kingdom of his Son he loves, in whom we have redemption, the forgiveness of sins.*

In the Ephesians passage Paul begins by describing the state of Gentiles before Christ--*you were separate from Christ, excluded from citizenship in Israel and foreigners to the covenants of the promise, without hope and without God in the world* (2:12). But now everything has changed, for *in Christ Jesus you who were once far away have been brought near through the blood of Christ. For he himself is our peace* who *has made the two [Jew and Gentile] one and has destroyed the barrier, the dividing wall of hostility* (2:13-14). Christ reconciled *both of them to*

God through the cross, by which he put to death their hostility (2:16). As a result of the cross of Jesus Christ, Gentiles have a new citizenship and a new identity and a new status. They are *no longer foreigners and aliens, but fellow citizens with God's people and members of God's household* (2;19).

It is in this context that Paul makes a statement that makes explicit much that he has implied--not only in Ephesians but throughout his letters -- *For through him [Christ] we both have access to the Father by one Spirit* (2:18). This parallels the statements of Jesus in the Gospel of John where we are invited to ask the Father anything in Jesus name.[44]

One of the things that distinguishes Christian prayer from that of non-Christian prayer is that the Christian does not expect God to come to our aid or answer us because of our need, or good deeds, or sincerity, or ritual, or even our love for God. Our access to God is because in love he took the initiative by sending Jesus Christ his Son to redeem us. Our access to God is because of *his glorious grace, which he has freely given us in the One he loves. In him [Christ] we have redemption through his blood, the forgiveness of sins, in accordance with the riches of God's grace that he lavished upon us* (Ephesians 1:6-8). *Because of his great love for us, God, who is rich in mercy, made us alive with Christ even when we were dead in transgressions--it is by grace you have been saved* (Ephesians 2:4-5). It is God himself who has made access to himself available, and he has done this through Jesus Christ.

The Christian therefore prays with confidence for *in him [Christ Jesus] and through faith in him we may approach God with freedom and confidence* (Ephesians 3:12).[45] Our access to God is through Jesus Christ. As Paul states in 1 Timothy 2:3-5, *For there is one God and one mediator between God and men, the man Christ Jesus, who gave himself as a ransom for all men.*[46] A mediator is an advocate, one who represents us. We come to God through Jesus Christ, and because of who he is and what he has done we can approach the eternal, holy God with the assurance of being welcomed.

The promises of God for blessing, protection, deliverance, and salvation in the Old Testament have their foundation in God's covenant promise to Abraham. The Apostle Paul shows that these promises belong to us in Christ. In Galatians he writes: *Christ redeemed us from the curse of the law by becoming a curse for us, for it is written: 'Cursed is everyone who is hung on a tree.' He redeemed us in order that the blessing given to Abraham might come to the Gentiles through Christ Jesus...*(Galatians 3:13-14). And in Romans he wrote: *The promise comes by faith, so that it may be by grace and may be guaranteed to all Abraham's offspring -- not only to those who are of the law but also to those who are of the faith of Abraham. He is the father of us all... He is our father in the sight of God, in whom he believed...* (Romans 4:16-17). And again: *If you belong to Christ, then you are Abraham's seed, and heirs according to the promise* (Galatians 3:29).

Through faith in Christ we can claim the promises of God made to the Old Testament saints, *For no matter how many promises God has made, they are 'Yes' in Christ. And so through him the 'Amen' is spoken by us to the glory of God* (2 Corinthians 1:20). When we dare to believe these promises and appropriate them for ourselves we are saying "the Amen" and glorify God. Through Jesus Christ we can pray with boldness and confidence.

Attitudes and Motives for Prayer

"Prayer is not only asking, but an attitude of mind which produces the atmosphere in which asking is perfectly natural."[47]

What is needed for prayer to be effective? Certainly it is not ritual, or using the right words or formula, nor is it the setting in which we pray or the intensity with which we pray or a particular position of our bodies. As God said to Samuel, *Man looks at the outward appearance, but the LORD looks at the heart* (1 Samuel 16:8). Again and again we are told in the scriptures that God knows our hearts. *The LORD searches every heart and understands every motive behind the thoughts* (1 Chronicles 28:9). ... *I the LORD search the heart and examine the mind...* (Jeremiah 17:18). These verses could be multiplied. So motives and attitudes are key factors in prayer that makes a difference. It has been observed that even faith is an attitude of mind.

In his occasional instructions on prayer Paul refers to attitudes and motives. In his prayer report in 2 Thessalonians 1, he adds the reason or motive that caused him to pray:

We pray this so that the name of our Lord Jesus may be glorified in you, and you in him, according to the grace of our God and the Lord Jesus Christ (2 Thessalonians 1:13).

When Paul states that he desires *the name of the Lord Jesus be glorified in you*, he means that their life style and the intentions of their heart honors the Lord and bears witness to his power to transform. When he writes that they in turn may be glorified in Christ, he means that they will be strengthened in faith and more and more reflect the character of their Lord. This can only be possible because God and the Lord Jesus Christ energizes them with his favor and grace. For Paul, everything is from God

It is because of him (God) that you are in Christ Jesus, who has become for us wisdom from God--that is our righteousness, holiness and redemption (1 Corinthians 1:30).

Christ has become our life (Colossians 3:4).

Another instruction which Paul gives is Colossians 4:2: *Devote yourselves to prayer, being watchful [in it] and thankful.* Prayer is not to be a haphazard, only when I have a need, kind of activity. It is to be intentional and regular. If prayer is all about us, then it is difficult when there is no pressing need to be devoted to it. However, if prayer is really about God -- his glory, his kingdom, his will, our desire to live in his presence and our acknowledgment of our dependence upon him -- then our being devoted, intentional and regular in it, is a necessity. The enemy of our soul would have us forget God. Intentional, regular prayer reinforces what we know in our hearts -- we really do need Christ if we are to be and do that which makes a difference (see John 15:1-8).

Paul, knowing our human weakness, adds two things to the idea of being devoted -- *being watchful [in it] and thankful.* For some unexplained reason the NIV omits the words *in it* which are in the Greek text. Gratitude, of course, is one of Paul's major themes in his letters and one of the impetus for prayer is certainly to acknowledge God's goodness to us. Gratitude causes us to be aware of the present moment. As has been said many times, the present moment is a gift, that is why it is called the present.

The admonition to be watchful and alert in prayer is exceedingly practical. It is so easy to go through the motions of prayer and realize that our minds have not been focused. One of the problems with intentional, regular, habitual prayer is that the good habit can become a dull routine which fails to engage the mind and the will. To watch in prayer means not only to be alert and alive while we pray, but also to be aware of the schemes of the devil and the signs of the times. We need to learn to see the kingdom of God issues in the news we read, see and hear so that our prayers truly reflect the heart of God.

Closely related to the attitude of gratefulness is being joyful and rejoicing. So it seems natural for Paul, in the context of the subject of prayer, to enjoin his readers to exhibit these attitudes. *Be joyful always; pray constantly; give thanks in all circumstances, for this is God's will for you in Christ Jesus* (1 Thessalonians 5:16-18). *Rejoice in the Lord always. I will say it again: Rejoice!. ... Do not be anxious about anything, but in everything, by prayer and petition, with thanksgiving, present your requests to God* (Philippians 4:4-6).

Rejoicing in the Lord and joyfulness and thanksgiving are forms of praise. It is somewhat surprising to me that Paul, for whom the Psalms and the praise of God in Israel's worship would be key elements of his heritage and training, never urges the readers of his letters to praise the Lord. His emphasis is upon living lives that bring honor to the Lord.

In 1 Timothy Paul urges purity of heart when he wrote, *I want men everywhere to lift up holy hands in prayer, without anger or disputing* (1 Timothy 2:8). In the ancient world, and especially in Judaism, the lifting of the hands in prayer was the traditional posture. It was a posture that symbolized both the greatness of God and the pray-ers willingness to receive.[48] When Paul urges the lifting up of *holy hands in prayer, without anger or disputing* he is urging the necessity of living righteous lives -- being in right relationship with God and the people around us. Our relationships with others effects our ability to truly pray. An unforgiving heart and bitterness of spirit blocks our being able to come into God's presence and receive his blessings.

PRAYER PRINCIPLE #8

We come to the Father through Jesus Christ

Paul often writes of God as *the God and Father of our Lord Jesus Christ.* What does it mean to you to think of God that way? Does this approach enrich or diminish your view of the God to whom you pray?

What effect does it have upon your confidence and expectations in prayer to realize that we come to God, not on the basis of our goodness or need, but through Jesus Christ?

Why can we claim the many promises in the Old Testament for ourselves today? Why is this not just wishful thinking?

Why are our attitudes and motives in prayer important? What attitudes in prayer do you need to cultivate and practice more?

Praying for Others

Although the Scriptures contain many examples of people praying for others (i.e., Abraham, Moses, Job, Psalms, Jesus, etc.), there are very few commands to pray for others. There is no such command in the Old Testament. The first time we are told to pray for others is when Jesus instructed us to *Pray for those who persecute you* (Matthew 5:44). In James 5:14 we are told to pray for the sick, and in 1 John 5:11 we are to pray for a fellow Christian who has committed sin. Other than these Paul is the only writer in the Bible that instructs us to pray for others and he does so three times.[49]

In Ephesians he wrote: *And pray in the Spirit on all occasions with all kinds of prayers and requests. With that in mind be alert and always keep on praying for all the saints. Pray also for me...* (Ephesians 6:18-19). In Colossians he wrote: *Devote yourselves to prayer, being watchful and thankful. And Pray for us, too...* (Colossians 4:2-3).

But the most far reaching instruction is found in 1 Timothy.

> *I urge, then, first of all, that requests, prayers, intercession and thanksgiving be made for everyone -- for kings and all those in authority, that we may live peaceful and quiet lives in all godliness and holiness. This is good, and pleases God our Savior, who wants all men to be saved and to come to a knowledge of the truth (1 Timothy 2:1-4).*

I would like to make two observations.

First, it is difficult to make clear distinctions in meaning for the various words Paul uses for prayer. What is clear is that he is encouraging prayer to be offered for everyone, especially kings and those in authority. This is a very broad mandate and implies that there is no one who is excluded from the influence of the prayers of God's people.

However, special attention is to be made toward those whose decisions and actions affect the well-being of many others. It is to the benefit of all that we are able to live peaceful and quiet lives rather than in circumstances, like war time, that force us to focus on self-preservation and the protection of those we love and for whom we are responsible.

Second, it is obvious that the prayers made should include our concern that those we pray for will come to the knowledge of the truth -- i.e., the gospel of God's saving love in Christ Jesus -- and so believe in Christ and experience salvation in all its dimensions.

In prayer for others, then, we become engaged in the battle against the darkness that blinds people's eyes and keeps them from seeing *the light of the gospel of the glory of Christ, who is the image of God* (2 Corinthians 4:4). In so doing we are attacking the very power and strongholds of the forces of darkness. In prayers for others we focus the light of God's love into the darkness of sin and unbelief.

I believe that in the name of our Lord Jesus Christ we should bind the forces of darkness that cause the blindness of unbelief in those for whom we pray.[50] Paul writes,

> *The weapons we fight with are not the weapons of the world. On the contrary, they have divine power to demolish strongholds. We demolish arguments and every pretension that sets itself up against the knowledge of God, and we take captive every thought to make it obedient to Christ (2 Corinthians 10:4-5).*

Certainly prayer is one of the weapons he used to destroy the strongholds of evil. Paul had a sense of authority because he knew who he was in Christ. In his great prayer in Ephesians 1, the Apostle prays that we may know the Father's *incomparably great power for us who believe.*

That power is like the working of his mighty strength, which he exerted in Christ when he raised him from the dead and seated him at his right hand in the heavenly realms, far above all rule and authority, power and dominion (i.e., all the forces of evil) … (Ephesians 1:19-21). But then in the second chapter he adds *And God raised us up with Christ and seated us with him in the heavenly realms in Christ Jesus* ... (Ephesians 2:6). We should note that this verse is not future tense -- something that God is going to do sometime -- but past tense -- something he has already done. This is speaking of a profound spiritual reality. Since Jesus is already seated at the Father's right hand and been given all authority over the forces of evil and since we have been seated with him, then through his authority and power we also have the right to take authority over the powers of darkness. As John says, *The reason the Son of God appeared was to destroy the devil's work* (1 John 3:8). Through the power of the Holy Spirit we are given the privilege of participating in Christ's redemptive ministry. This may be the new frontier in our learning to pray.

One Other Instruction[51]

Paul gives one other instruction for prayer which I wanted to ignore but in light of the purpose of this book must include. 1 Corinthians 11:3-16 is a difficult passage for us in the western world to relate to. The setting is instructions regarding worship.

> *Now I want you to realize that the head of every man is Christ, and the head of the woman is man, and the head of Christ is God. Every man who prays or prophesies with his head covered dishonors his head. And every woman who prays or prophesies with her head uncovered dishonors her head--it is just as though her head were shaved. If a woman does not cover her head, she should have her hair cut off; and if it is a disgrace for a woman to have her hair cut or shaved off, she should cover her head. A man ought not to cover his head, since he is the image and glory of God; but the woman is the glory of man. For man did not come from woman, but woman from man. For this reason, and because of the angels, the woman ought to have a sign of authority on her head.*

In the Lord, however, woman is not independent of man, nor is man independent of woman. For as woman came from man, so also man is born of woman. But everything comes from God. Judge for yourselves: Is it proper for a woman to pray to God with her head uncovered? Does not the very nature of things teach you that if a man has long hair, it is a disgrace to him, but that if a woman has long hair, it is her glory? For long hair is given to her as a covering. If anyone wants to be contentious about this, we have no other practice--nor do the churches of God (1 Corinthians 11:3-16).

A couple of observations:

First, this appears to be instructions that are determined by the culture. I doubt that he would have written these instructions to the church at Rome, for women had a different status in the Roman society. There is, however, an important principle involved: we need to be culturally sensitive in our expression of our faith and exercise of our freedom. Sometimes it is the messenger rather than the gospel message that is the barrier to a people hearing the good news of God's love in Christ Jesus. I remember when we sent a mission team to a South American country, it was with the explicit instructions that the females could not wear slacks or shorts because of the cultural traditions of the people among whom they were to work.

Cultural sensitivity was important to Paul. So just before he wrote this section, he wrote:

Do not cause anyone to stumble, whether Jews, Greeks or the church of God--even as I try to please everybody in every way. For I am not seeking my own good but the good of many, so that they may be saved. Follow my example, as I follow the example of Christ (1 Corinthians 10:32-11:1).

Again he writes, *We put no stumbling block in anyone's path, so that our ministry will not be discredited* (2 Corinthians 6:3). At the conclusion of explaining his philosophy of ministry he writes, *I have become all things to all men so that by all possible means I might save some. I do all this for the sake of the gospel...* (1 Corinthians 9:22-23). And to the Romans he writes about being sensitive with regard to eating and drinking:

> *Do not destroy the work of God for the sake of food. All food is clean, but it is wrong for a man to eat anything that causes someone else to stumble. It is better not to eat meat or drink wine or to do anything else that will cause your brother to fall (Romans 14:20-21).*

There is a fine line between being culturally sensitive and compromise. We need the wisdom and grace of God to enable us to discern how we are to act in various settings where experience and assumptions are different from our own. As a young seminarian I worked with children in the slums of Chicago. The first instruction I was given was to never speak of God as Father because most of the children with whom we worked either did not know who their father was or had such a bad experience with their father that the very word carried a negative content which built a barrier to their understanding the gospel message. We needed to build a bridge and provide good models before introducing the concept of God as our Father in heaven.

The second observation is simply that if we are unwilling to submit to authority, this unwillingness, this pride, will short circuit our prayers so that they are ineffective. Anyone who would be a leader must also be willing to submit to the leadership of others and be a supportive follower. Paul writes: *Submit to one another out of reverence for Christ* (Ephesians 5:21). And in Philippians he instructs us: *Do nothing out of selfish ambition or vain conceit, but in humility consider others better than yourselves. Each of you should look not only to your own interests, but also to the interests of others* (Philippians 2:3-4). The submission of humility is a key attitude in our relationship with God and with our brothers and sisters in the church, and one of the most difficult for us to learn.

Paul knew that there were some who might reject these instructions. Sometimes when we have new understandings, we tend to rush to put them into practice. Paul's word is a cautionary word to the whole church to make changes slowly when they run counter to the surrounding culture.

PRAYER PRINCIPLE #9

The cultural setting for our witness to Christ may demand lifestyle adjustments on our part.

Someone has observed that frequently our prayers for others can be reduced to "Make them like us!" How might being more culturally sensitive (i.e., to teenagers, the poor, those of a different religious background etc.) help us to pray more meaningfully?

One of the great changes in evangelism in other countries in the last twenty years has been the encouragement of worship and prayer to be in the style of the culture, rather than simply importing and translating our hymns and praise songs. What is the danger of adapting the expressions of faith to another culture? How can we be certain that it is only the expressions of faith and not the essence of the gospel that is being adapted?

PART THREE

A FRESH LOOK AT THE SALUTATIONS

SECTION 1: The Salutations as an Apostolic Blessing

I. The Form and function of the Salutations

There was an established standard form for writing letters in the ancient world. The Apostle Paul follows this established form, which can be easily seen in his letter to Philemon.

The author identified himself v. 1

The address: the name of the person or persons to whom the letter is written v. 1-2

The greeting or salutation v. 3

Thanksgiving v. 1-7. Although this is often a part of the Greek letter form, it was also frequently omitted, especially in a business letter. (see Acts 23:26-30, The letter of James. Paul omits the thanksgiving in two letters: Galatians and Titus.).

The body of the letter vv. 8-22

The conclusion vv. 23-24 This might include greetings from other people

The closing v. 25 which often expresses some kind of well wishes

The Apostle Paul greatly enlarges the normal Greek greeting. While the normal Greek salutation was *charein,* usually translated "greetings" (cf. Acts 15:23; 23:26; James 1:1), Paul's salutations are more involved: *Grace to you and peace from God our Father and the Lord Jesus Christ.*

What I want to do is explore possible reasons why Paul wrote such an extended salutation, what it means and how our prayer experiences might be enriched by them. In this section, I will argue that Paul has changed the simple greeting so that it has become an apostolic blessing.

I am struck by the fact that all the salutations in Paul's letters (except 1 Thessalonians) are "*from God the (*or *our) Father and the Lord Jesus Christ*" or something very similar. Paul is not simply giving the common greeting, nor is this simply a "Christianized" formula replacing the common greeting. The very form of the salutations lead me to consider them as intentionally crafted in the form of a blessing which Paul wishes to give to his readers. Paul very intentionally conveys a blessing from God and Jesus. He is the conduit, the channel through which this blessing is conveyed.

When one considers Paul's greetings with that of other writers of the New Testament, one is impressed by the fact that 1 Peter and Jude, along with 1 Thessalonians have a "Christianized" greeting which is from the author.[52] The three letters which have a greeting similar to Paul's (2 Peter, 2 John, and Revelations) are probably influenced by and indebted to Paul for their extended greetings since each of the writers would be acquainted with Paul's letters.[53]

II. What is a "Blessing?"

When I say that this is an apostolic blessing, what do I mean?[54] How does one define a blessing? The Greek word translated "bless" in the New Testament is *eulogeo* (from which we get our word "eulogize"), which literally means to speak good words, and conveys the meaning "to bestow a blessing," "to act graciously toward," and "to praise." The idea of blessing is somewhat complex. When parents give their blessing to a marriage, it means that they give their approval. When we say to someone, "The Lord bless you," we mean something like: "May God meet all your needs and give you success in what you do." When we say that something has blest us, we mean that in some way our lives have been enriched. While to bless someone may simply mean to say good things to or about them, in the salutations Paul is not saying nice things about the recipients of the letter, nor is he simply expressing his wish for the recipients,[55] but rather he is conveying something from God the Father and the Lord Jesus Christ, namely grace and peace.

III. The Salutations as an Apostolic Blessing

When I call the greetings an apostolic blessing, I do so because I believe that Paul understands himself as standing in the priestly tradition of the Old Testament when he conveys this blessing. This seems to be confirmed by what he wrote in Romans 15:15 -16:

> *I have written you quite boldly on some points, as if to remind you of them again, because of the grace God gave me to be a minister of Christ Jesus to the Gentiles with the priestly duty of proclaiming the gospel of God, so that the Gentiles might become an offering acceptable to God, sanctified by the Holy Spirit.*

And in verse 29 he can say, *I know that when I come to you, I will come in the full measure of the blessing of Christ.* Paul considers the privilege of preaching to the Gentiles as a priestly function. One of the functions of the priest was to bless the people in the name of the Lord.

This tradition of blessing the people goes back to Numbers 6:22-27:

> *The LORD said toMoses, "Tell Aaron and his sons, This is how you are to bless the Israelites. Say to them: 'The LORD bless you and keep you; the LORD make his face shine upon you and be gracious to you; the LORD turn his face toward you and give you peace.' " So they will put my name on the Israelites, and I will bless them.*

Do not miss the emphasis: although the blessing is pronounced by the priests, the blessing comes from the LORD. The priest is simply the conduit God uses to convey the blessing. The spoken blessing is a reminder to the people that they are dependent on God. But without God's confirming action the blessing is only so many words.

Paul [and also Peter (2 Peter 1:2) and John (2 John 3; Revelations 1:4-5) who use a similar formula] can pronounce this blessing from God and

Jesus because he is an apostle -- an official and authoritative representative of Jesus Christ, and a servant of the gospel. It is apparent from his letters that he sensed a special responsibility, a "grace," to bless others as part of his authority as an apostle of the Lord Jesus Christ. There is a sense in which those who have been called and ordained by our Lord for special service, such as pastors and missionaries, etc., have a unique authority and responsibility to convey to others the grace and gifts of God. It is not that they are more holy than everyone else, but rather because God in his sovereignty has chosen them to be his official representatives.

The authority resides in the call and the office rather than in the individual. The Scriptures make it clear that they will be judged with greater strictness for what they have done with the opportunities God has given them. They are simply stewards of the grace of God and it is expected of stewards -- those who are entrusted with the responsibility to manage what belongs to another-- that they be faithful (1 Corinthians 4:2).

IV. The Privilege of God's People -- blessing others

While this is a special responsibility of one who stands in the priestly tradition, there is another tradition which runs through the Scripture. In the patriarchal narratives especially, we find that the father pronounced a blessing upon his sons and in Exodus 19:5-6 God announces that the whole nation is to be a kingdom of priests: *Although the whole earth is mine, you will be for me a kingdom of priests and a holy nation.* In 1 Peter 2:9, Peter states that this is true also for the followers of Jesus.

In the Old Testament priests were anointed with oil, a sign of the Holy Spirit. In the New Testament the followers of Christ are also anointed with the Holy Spirit. In fact, the distinguishing mark of the followers of Christ is that they are the bearers of the Holy Spirit who dwells within them. This means that the true followers of Christ always represent Christ and bring the Spirit of Christ with them wherever they go. They have the privilege of bringing a blessing on everyone their life touches.

In Galatians 3:14 Paul writes, *He redeemed us in order that the blessing given to Abraham might come to the Gentiles through Christ Jesus, so that by faith we might receive the promise of the Spirit.* It is interesting and important to note that even though there is no mention of the Spirit in the original promise, Paul understands the gift of the Holy Spirit to be the fulfillment of God's promise to Abraham. The Spirit is the ultimate blessing which enables the believer to be a full participant in the promise and the blessing: *I will bless you and you will be a blessing*. The promise-blessing which God made to Abraham becomes a present reality in the life of the believer: *I will make you into a great nation and I will bless you: I will make your name great and you will be a blessing. I will bless those who bless you and whoever curses you I will curse; and all peoples on earth will be blessed through you* (Genesis 12:2-3).[56]

This covenant with Abraham is repeated 5 times in Genesis, but in a shortened form which indicates the most important aspects, namely, *I will bless you and you will be a blessing -- through you all peoples on earth will be blessed.*

In this abridged form the promise is repeated and affirmed, often in paraphrased form some 395 times in the Old and New Testaments.[57] Paul makes it clear that believers in Christ become spiritual heirs of Abraham and can claim the promise God made to Abraham as theirs: *I will bless you and make you a blessing.*

When one looks at the New Testament witness, it becomes very clear that the responsibility of blessing others is not the exclusive privilege of the apostles or even of the leaders of the congregation. So Paul can write:

I long see you so that I may impart to you some spiritual gift to make you strong--that is, that you and I may be mutually encouraged by each other's faith. (Rom. 1:11-12.) Paul will not only be a blessing to the Romans, he will also receive blessings from them.

When one considers the instructions given regarding life in the community of the followers of Christ, it becomes apparent that each Christian has the responsibility of enriching the lives of all the others. Note these representative passages.

> *In Christ we who are many form one body, and each member belongs to all the others. We have different gifts, according to the grace given us. (Romans 12:5)*

Your love has given me great joy and encouragement, because you, brother, have refreshed the hearts of the saints. (Philemon 7)

Accept one another, then, just as Christ accepted you, in order to bring praise to God...I myself am convinced, my brothers, that you yourselves are full of goodness, complete in knowledge and competent to instruct one another. (Romans 15:7, 14)

Now to each one the manifestation of the Spirit is given for the common good. (1 Corinthians 12:7)

Therefore encourage one another and build each other up, just as in fact you are doing. (1 Thessalonians 5:11)

These few verses could easily be multiplied. What is clear is that salvation is not just something between the believer and the Lord, but involves the responsibility to live in community as a positive, contributing member, blessing others by who we are and what we do. [58]

In his small volume, *The Power of a Blessing,* Eugene Peterson writes:

> "A blessing is powerful. Blessings offer us comfort, protection, hope, vision--and even more. They represent God's best for us as his people. In a blessing, we are drawn into his plan and passion for our future.
>
> Whether God blesses us or we bless one another, the power of a blessing lies in the One who truly gives the blessing: *God.* A blessing would be nearly fruitless if it relied merely on the power of the spoken word or the earnestness of the heart to move it from desire to reality, as if it were an incantation or a spell. The blessings that we speak can in fact bless other people because God allows them to bless other people. He actively 'agrees' with us as we affirm his promises.
>
> In that way, our relationship to him also has great power. God agrees with us and carries out our requests in part because of our position--of

both blesser and blessed--as his children, whom he loves deeply. When God, or someone who speaks God's words, offer a blessing, it is almost as if the blesser is saying, 'May you, as one who belongs to God, experience this: God's best.'

A blessing is powerful because it aligns with God's will....

Blessings allow us the opportunity to take hold of God's willingness. They help us to participate with God in the best he has for us, moving closer to his greatest desires for us -- even when those desires simply involve obedience on our part....

Consistent with his character, God allows us to participate in his great plan as we bless one another...

When God blesses us, as he moves us more into his will, our identity is redefined. We become more like him, more like the people he longs for us to be. And in that way, a blessing is nearly a biblical naming ceremony, calling us out of our present selves to lay hold of his bigger plan -- as when God blesses Jacob and renames him Israel (Genesis 32:22-32)...God blesses us and affirms our relationship with him, redefining us and making us more like him, taking us even further into his great story. ..."[59]

V. Sharing our story with one another

Through the years my life has been blessed by others. As a small boy about 10 or 12 years of age, an old retired and feeble former pastor laid his hands on my head and prayed that God would bless me and make me a blessing to others. I'm sure Rev. Lambert did not consider this a great thing for him to do, but for me...I could never forget that prayer and the sense I had that God had touched me through him.

I have had lay persons who through a touch, a word, a prayer or an act have been God's instrument to bless me. Many times I have felt like Pontipher, the captain of the palace guards of whom we read, *The Lord blessed the household of the Egyptian because of Joseph.* (Genesis 39:5).

God has blessed me because of others.

Whenever I have sensed that God had used me to bring a blessing to another person's life, it has been a cause, not for pride, but rather of wonder and humility. I think this sense of wonder and delight is caught by the rendering of Romans 15:18-19 in the Living Bible: *I dare not judge how effectively he* [Christ] *has used others, but I know this: he has used me to win the Gentiles to God. I have won them by my message and by the good way I have lived before them, and by the miracles done through me as signs from God--all by the Holy Spirit's power. In this way I have preached the full Gospel of Christ...*

As Christians we are the representatives of Christ, the Holy Spirit living inside us, and we are to live not for ourselves but for him who loved us gave himself for us. We are to be people who strive in all we do to serve the Lord and the result is that others are blessed because of us. Remember the promise: *I will bless you and you will be (not might be) a blessing.*

Our prayer life should be impacted by this conviction that God has called us to be a blessing to others. Although there are many general blessings which God gives automatically to everyone -- i.e. He sends his rain on the righteous and the wicked (Matthew 5:44) -- there are other special blessings which come because of prayer. A picture that has helped me is that of a magnifying glass. Although the sun shines brightly so that the whole earth is illuminated, one can take a magnifying glass and focus the sun's rays so that they can start a fire. The magnifying glass does only one thing -- focus the sun's rays. The energy to start the fire comes from the sun, not the glass. I picture my prayers for others as that magnifying glass which focuses God's love specifically on the person for whom I pray. It has often been noted that there are some things which God only does in response to prayer. It is not as though we had to tell God what to do, for often we do not know what another person really needs. All we need to do is to hold the other person up so that the healing love of God can be focused and His power released to meet their needs.

The power of a blessing lies not only in its ability to connect one to God but also in its reminding us of who we are and of God's gifts and goodness to us. A blessing can also serve as a challenge to growth as it inspires one to understand and reach out to realize God's purpose for us.

Although there are many prayers recorded in the Bible, i.e., the book of Psalms, prayers of Moses, Daniel, etc., the prayers in Paul's letters are unique for these prayers are not for himself, and very few are brought forth because of some circumstance, but rather reflect his prayers for the spiritual welfare of his readers. The only other account in the Bible of someone telling another the content of what they prayed for them is Jesus' statement to Peter in Luke 22:31-32.

However, the Apostle Paul's letters are peppered with prayers and reports of the contents of his prayers for others. Have you ever wondered why Paul records the substance of the prayers he prays for the various people who receive his letters? It is not necessary that they know what he has prayed--after all, the prayer is to God and not them. I believe there are at least four reasons why Paul, knowing the power of blessing, records the content of his prayers.

1. They assure the recipients of Paul's care and concern for them; he is standing with them and assisting them in their spiritual struggles.

2. They are a reminder of God's purpose for them

3. They serve as a reminder and challenge for the recipients to *grow in the grace and knowledge of our Lord Jesus Christ* (2 Peter 3:18).

4. It gives an illustration of how they can pray for the spiritual welfare of others. Most people's prayers for others is focused primarily on the physical and situational needs. These prayers give another paradigm for praying for others that illustrates how we can give depth and breadth to our intercessions.

When we look at the salutations -- *Grace to you and peace from God our Father and the Lord Jesus Christ* -- we discover that they are a short summary of what is most basic and distinctive in the gospel of Jesus Christ. Because of the gospel there are four new perspectives which shape the Christ-followers understand of him/herself. The gospel gives us:

1. A new understanding of salvation -- grace and peace
2. A new understanding of God -- he is the/our Father
3. A new understanding of who Jesus is -- He is Lord
4. A new understanding of ourselves as disciples of Jesus -- we are servants

Applying the concept of Blessing: Prayer Principle # 10

We are to be person's who are aware of how others have enriched our lives and who are committed to enriching the lives of others.

1. Share briefly on experience you have had of someone who has blessed you.

2. Share briefly a time when God has used you to bless someone. How did it make you feel?

3. Discuss how we, in our particular stage of life, can be a conduit of God's blessing to others. How does our blessing others change according to the stage of life we are in?

Section II: THE SALUTATIONS AS A SUMMARY OF THAT WHICH IS MOST DISTINCTIVE IN THE CHRISTIAN FAITH

A NEW UNDERSTANDING OF SALVATION

When we understand that the salutations of the Apostle Paul's letters are really an apostolic blessing, it is not hard to see how they encapsulate that which is most distinctive in the Christian faith. When one understands and accepts the gospel of Jesus Christ it means that they have a new understanding of God, and a new understanding of Jesus, a new understanding of who we are in Christ, and a new understanding of Salvation.

Although the normal Greek address "greetings", and Paul's "grace", come from the same Greek word root, it is an extremely shallow interpretation to conclude that all Paul does is to "christianize" the greeting and add the Jewish, "shalom," which means "peace." Rather by placing these two words together, he is giving a summary of the distinctive Christian view of the salvation which comes from God, the Father and the Lord, Jesus Christ.

Grace

The basic idea underlying the word grace is, to use a favorite definition, "God's unmerited favor." The idea is of a gift that is kindly and mercifully given to one who does not deserve it. So another popular definition is that "Grace is God dealing with us, not as we deserve but according to our need." In the New Testament, grace is very closely aligned with Jesus' sacrificial death on our behalf. Thus another popular definition is that grace is "**G**od's **R**iches **At** **C**hrist's **E**xpense.'

Although the most common interpretation of grace is that of undeserved favor and kindness, the Greek word is used with meanings that are sometimes quite different. Because a person who receives a gift is grateful, ten times in Paul's letters it simply means "thanks" (i.e., "Thanks to God," Romans 7:25 et. al.). The word can be used to refer to the offering for the poor in Jerusalem which Paul is receiving from the Gentile churches (i.e., 2 Corinthians 6, 7 et. al.). Paul can instruct the Colossians (4:6), *Let your conversation be always full of grace, seasoned with salt, so that you may know how to answer everyone*. Because we have received grace our speech and lives are to marked by graciousness rather than defensive, self-serving behavior. There are other meanings which we will try to bring out in what follows.[60]

Grace is one of Paul's favorite terms. Of its 156 occurrences in the New Testament, it is found 112 times in the Pauline literature. This is a favorite term of the Apostle because it expresses so succinctly his own experience. As he wrote in 1 Corinthians 15:8-10, in a section that is summarizing the gospel with special reference to the resurrection: *Last of all, as to one untimely born, he [Jesus] appeared also to me. For I am the least of the apostles, unfit to be called an apostle, because I persecuted the church of God. But by the grace of God I am what I am, and his grace toward me was not in vain. On the contrary, I worked harder than any of them, though it was not I, but the grace of God which is with me.*

In verse 10 Paul uses "grace' three times with at least two distinct meanings. *But by the grace [kindness, mercy, favor] of God I am what I am, and his grace [favor, mercy, kindness] toward me was not in vain.* The first two occasions of the word grace the primary meaning seems to be that God's action in revealing Jesus to him on the Damascus road was in no way dependent on Paul. It was simply God's great mercy and kindness, all of which was undeserved. The third use of the term "grace" in this verse, however, seems to mean something more. It does not make sense to understand *I worked harder than any of them -- though it was not I, but the [undeserved mercy, favor, kindness] of God which is with me.* This time the word "grace" is more dynamic and seems to imply something that energizes and makes effective one's efforts. Although the word grace is not used, Philippians 2:12-13 come to mind, *Work out your own salvation with fear and trembling; for God is at work in you, both to will and to work for his good pleasure.* The writer to the Hebrews (13:9) tells us that *It is good for our hearts to be strengthened by grace...* The concept of grace is not limited to the idea of undeserved favor but implies as well that God is actively working to fill up what is lacking in our lives.

In Ephesians 3 the word is used with still another nuance: *For this reason I, Paul...assuming that you have heard of the stewardship of God's grace that was given to me for you, how the mystery was made known to me by revelation...Of this gospel I was made a minister according to the gift of God's grace which was given me by the working of his power. To me, though I am the very least of all the saints, this grace was given, to preach to the Gentiles the unsearchable riches of Christ... (Eph 3:1-3, 7-8).* In this passage Paul uses the word "grace" to refer to his call to be an apostle to the Gentiles. It means "favor" yet something more definite, it means God's favor which resulted in Paul's call to preach the gospel to the Gentiles. "Grace" here equals "Call" or "Apostleship". Note that it *was given me by the working of his power*. Grace and energy are very closely aligned.

The concept of grace has been a difficult doctrine for the church to hold on to. It goes against all the natural inclinations of our being. We would like to think that in some way we can earn or deserve a right relationship with God and the reward of heaven. Grace, however, means that it is God who takes the initiative and that salvation is all a gift of

God's compassionate love. I read somewhere, that Karl Barth once said that in the Incarnation, -- i.e., God sent his only Son into the world and 'the Word became flesh'-- that God was saying to us, "I refuse to be God apart from you." When Jesus took on our humanity he did not put it on as we might dress up in a costume for Halloween, only to take it off when the party is over. When Jesus took on our humanity he became man forever -- this is part of the meaning of the resurrection of the body. As Ireneus, an early church father once said: "Now there is a little bit of the dust of earth on the throne of heaven." This was an act of pure grace, not prompted by our desire for God but rather by God's love and desire for us which caused him to send *his own Son in the likeness of sinful man to be a sin offering* (Romans 8:3).

Many years ago I was given an outline using the letters G R A C E which has helped me understand and appreciate the richness of God's wonderful grace. What follows is a short meditation. Focusing on Ephesians 1 and 2 we can draw the following understanding of Grace.

G= Gift -- the Principle

Paul writes: *For by grace you have been saved through faith; and this is not your own doing, it is the gift of God--not because of works, lest any man should boast.* (Eph. 2:8-9).

Salvation is a gift which we receive by faith. Faith is not a merit, it is simply believing what God has said is true and accepting his gift on the basis of what Jesus Christ has done for us. In the New Testament faith always includes three aspects: 1) the content, what is believed; 2) trust, a willingness to entrust one's life to God; and 3) obedience, the acting on the belief and trust. Faith is our acceptance of God's gift. We are saved by grace through faith.

One reason that our best efforts can not earn our acceptance with God is that good works are the currency of earth, while faith is the currency of heaven. Let me give a simple illustration. Suppose that you decided to buy a new coat and found one you liked for $400 dollars. You want to pay cash for it so you go home and from a box on the closet shelf you take out four crisp one hundred dollar bills. Now you have the money for the coat. But there is a problem, the money you hold in your hand is monopoly money -- good when you are playing monopoly but try to buy that coat with that play money! The question is not do you have $400, you hold four crisp $100 bills in your hand; but rather what currency is accepted. It is not that our good works are worthless, though the scripture does say that our righteousness is like filthy rags to God (like monopoly money to a merchant). Good works are the currency of earth; but the currency of heaven is faith in Jesus Christ and his sacrifice for our sins.

Oswald Chambers observed:

"The Gospel of the grace of God awakens an intense longing in human souls and an equally intense resentment, because the revelation which it brings is not palatable. There is a certain pride in man that will give and give, but to come and accept is another thing. I will give myself in consecration, I will do anything, but do not humiliate me to the level of the most hell-deserving sinner and tell me that all I have to do is to accept the gift of salvation through Jesus Christ.

We have to realize that we cannot earn or win anything from God; we must either receive it as a gift or do without it. The greatest blessing spiritually is the knowledge that we are destitute; until we get there our Lord is powerless. He can do nothing for us if we think we are sufficient of ourselves; we have to enter into His Kingdom through the door of destitution. As long as we are rich, possessed of anything in the way of pride or independence, God cannot do anything for us. It is only when we get hungry spiritually that we receive the Holy Spirit. The gift of the essential nature of God is made effectual in us by the Holy Spirit; He imparts to us the quickening life of Jesus…"[61]

Salvation is a gift which we receive by faith. There is a beautiful picture of this in the movie version of Victor Hugo's *Les Miserables*. Jean val Jean has just been released from 19 years hard labor. He is sent home on probation. He is tired and hungry and stops at a priest's residence to ask for food. Instead he is brought in and given a meal and invited to stay the night. During the night he wakes up and decides take the silver in the house and escape. The next day the police bring him back saying that they had searched Jean val Jean and found the silver and that he had said the priest had given it to him. The old priest responds that that was true, and while the police are having some wine, the old priest puts his hands on

Jean val Jean's shoulder and says, Jean val Jean, you promised to become a new man. Now I have given you back your life and now I give you to God.

Jean val Jean got what he did not deserve. It was mercy but it was more. The old priest took the loss and gave him back his life. That is what God has done in Jesus Christ. And it is grace. The Apostle Paul could never forget that he had been a persecutor of the church and an enemy of Christ, when God reached down to him, and he was given the revelation of the risen Lord Jesus and called to be the Apostle to the Gentiles. It was undeserved. It was a gift…it was grace.

R = Redemption -- the Price

Paul writes: In him we redemption through his blood, the forgiveness of our trespasses, according to the riches of his grace which he lavished upon us (Eph. 1:7-8).

Redemption means to buy back at a price. Grace is free, but not cheap. God paid a great price, he *loved the world so much that he gave his only Son that whoever believes in him should not perish but have eternal life* (John 3:16). And in Romans 8:32 Paul writes of the Father *who spared not his own Son but gave him up for us all…* The price of redeeming grace was great to the Father and costly for the Son. Paul can write of *the Son of God, who loved me and gave himself for me* (Gal. 2:20).

We would be rewarded if we would consider deeply what it meant to the Father not to spare his own Son and what it meant to the Son not to be spared but to become a sin offering for mankind.

The sacrifice of Jesus Christ is set forth in the great hymn of Phil 2 in which our Lord is described as he *who, though he was in the form of God, did not count equality with God a thing to be grasped, but emptied himself, taking the form of a servant, being born in the likeness of men. And being found in human form he humbled himself and became obedient unto death, even death on a cross* (Phil. 2:6-8).

An old gospel song asks: "Why should he love me so? Why should my Savior to Calvary go? Why should he love me so?"

The price and the purpose of grace is redemption.

A = Access and Adoption -- the Privilege

Paul writes of the privilege of prayer: *through him [Christ] we both have access in one Spirit to the Father (Eph. 2:18).* Because of God's amazing grace we have free access at anytime, in any place and under any circumstances. We do not need to go through a "secretary," pastor, priest or any other person. *For there is one God and there is one mediator between God and men, the man Christ Jesus, who gave himself as a ransom for all...* (1 Timothy 2:5,6). To the Romans he writes that, *through him [Christ] we have obtained access to this grace in which we stand, and we rejoice in our hope of sharing the glory of God (Romans 5:2).* We have the privilege of coming into God's presence through Jesus Christ our Lord.

When we approach God in prayer, we do not come as beggars or "party crashers" who have no right to be there, We come as his children, we belong to him! That is why the Apostle tells us *In [Christ] and through faith in him we may approach God with freedom and confidence* (Eph. 3:12). Grace changes our position in relation to God from an outsider to one who is a member of the family.

"A" also stands for Adoption. *In love he predestined us to be adopted as his sons [children] through Jesus Christ, in accordance with his pleasure and will--to the praise of his glorious grace, which he has freely given us in the One he loves* (Eph. 1:5-6). This is an important concept for Paul. It means that those who did not belong to the family of God have been adopted, brought into the family, and now have all the privileges that belong to one who was born into the family. We are now heirs with Christ (Ro. 8:15). I repeat what I just said: We do not come to God crawling as one who has no right to be in his presence, no, we come boldly because we are his children through Jesus Christ, and we belong.

I have two children, both of whom are adopted. When I adopted them they became my children and I was responsible to provide for them, care and love them. My wife and I often gave thanks to God for the young mothers who made a great sacrifice of love by giving their child to us. I could never be neutral with regard to abortion, because my children could just as easily never have been born. My children have brought great joy and delight to my wife and I. Although they each have a natural mother and father, they are my children and I am their father. They belong to me. So it is spiritually. Through Christ, God has brought us into his family, and we are now his children. As Peter puts it in his first letter,

> *Once you were no people but now you are God's people; once you had not received mercy but now you have received mercy (1 Peter 2:10).*

All of this is because of God's amazing grace.

C = Character -- the Product

Paul writes: *For we are God's workmanship created in Christ Jesus to do good works, which God prepared in advance for us to do* (Eph. 2:10). And in Romans 5 he speaks of rejoicing in our hope of sharing the glory of God, and also rejoicing in suffering because it produces endurance which in turn produces character and character produces hope.

When God saves us through his grace, he not only forgives us but we are also given the Holy Spirit, who is a guarantee of our inheritance. The purpose is that we might live to the praise of his glory (Eph. 1:13-14). Grace is more than God's favor, it is also his mighty energy. My favorite definition of grace comes from John Henry Jowett as quoted by my homiletics professor 40 years ago: "Grace is more than mercy, yea more than tender mercy. Grace is more than kindness, yea more than loving kindness. Grace is the energy of divine holiness, issuing forth in love toward the unlovely, to create in the unlovely His own loveliness."

This reality of God's intention that we be created anew in the loveliness of his character displayed in Jesus Christ is set forth in Romans 8:29, *Those whom God foreknew, he also predestined to be conformed to the likeness of his Son, that he might be the firstborn among many brethren.* And so for Paul the only thing that really counts *is a new creation* (Gal. 6:15). God's intention for us is not only that we should share all eternity in his presence but that we would develop into the likeness of the character of our Lord. This happens on the anvil of life's hardships and challenges, as we learn to trust him and obey him and serve him.

Our character is displayed by our moral and ethical behavior and by how we relate to others. Because we are the recipients of God's marvelous grace, and have experienced his kindness, mercy and acceptance, we in turn have an obligation to be people who extend grace -- undeserved kindness, mercy, forgiveness, love, and acceptance -- to those around us. By the power of his grace working in us through the Holy Spirit we are called and empowered to live holy lives in an unholy world. In the words of a song that was popular a few years ago: "They will know we are Christians by our love, by our love. They will know we are Christians by our love."

E = Eternity -- the Prospect

Paul writes, *And God raised us up with Christ and seated us with him in the heavenly realms in Christ Jesus, in order that in the coming ages he might show the incomparable riches of his grace, expressed in his kindness to us in Christ Jesus* (Eph. 2:6-7). For the child of God, "the best is yet to be." We have a future all sublime and eternity is not darkness but light and joy in the presence of our Lord.

I was talking with a friend recently and he conveyed something that he had heard that had intrigued him. He had heard a preacher say: "Eternity is an expanding of what now is." What an intriguing thought! If we allow the negative things to take root in our spirit--bitterness, anger, jealousy, hatred, and the like--they will just keep expanding in eternity. If now they have the ability to destroy our happiness and well-being -- just think of the misery they will bring to us if they were to expand for ever and ever! But if we allow God to cleanse our hearts through Christ's sacrifice, he will cause the beautiful fruit of the Spirit to grow -- *love, joy, peace, patience, kindness, goodness, faithfulness, gentleness and self-control* -- these also will expand throughout eternity. If they bring joy to us now, just think of the gladness which will be ours as the beautiful things of the spirit multiply.

Max Lucado addresses this when he wrote:

"Of all the blessings of heaven, one of the greatest will be you! You will be God's *magnum opus,* His work of art. The angels will gasp. God's work will be completed. At last, you will have a heart like His. You will love with a perfect love. You will worship with a radiant face. You'll hear each word God speaks. Your heart will be pure, your words will be like jewels, your thoughts will be like treasures. You will be just like Jesus. You will, at long last, have a heart like His. Envision the heart of Jesus and you'll be envisioning your own. Guiltless. Fearless. Thrilled and joyous. Tirelessly worshiping. Flawlessly discerning. As the mountain stream is pristine and endless, so will be your heart. You will be like Him."[62]

It may be important to note one last thing about grace. It is almost always predicated as God's grace. However there are a few exceptions where the grace of Christ is referred to: 2 Corinthians 8:9, 12:9 and 13:13, and Ephesians 4:7 and 1 Timothy 1:12-14.

> *You know the grace of our Lord Jesus Christ, that though he was rich, yet for your sakes he became poor, so that you through his poverty might become rich. (2 Corinthians. 8:9)*

> *But he [the Lord] said to me, My grace is sufficient for you, for my power is made perfect in weakness. Therefore I will boast all the more gladly about my weaknesses, so that Christ's power may rest on me. (2 Corinthians 12:9)*

> *May the grace of the Lord Jesus Christ, and the love of God and the fellowship of the Holy Spirit be with you all. (2 Corinthians 13:13)*

> *But to each one of us grace has been given as Christ apportioned it. (Ephesians 4:7).*

> *I thank Christ Jesus our Lord, who has given me strength, that he considered me faithful, appointing me to his service. Even though I was once a blasphemer and a persecutor and a violent man, I was shown mercy because I acted in ignorance and unbelief. The grace of our Lord was poured out on me abundantly, along with the faith and love that are in Christ Jesus. (1 Timothy 1:12-14)*

It is interesting that John concludes the Revelation with this benediction: *The grace of the Lord Jesus be with God's people. Amen. (Rev. 22:21)*

The grace of Christ is not different from the grace of God. That Paul could speak of the grace of Christ indicates the phenomenal reality that Paul thinks of Christ as in some way equal with the Father.

Peace

Paul completely transformed the normal greeting into a shorthand statement of the essence of the Christian faith and a conveyance of blessing upon his readers. Taking off from the normal "greeting," he changed it to "grace to you." But he went further and added "and peace." In so doing he brought the greeting into the arena of the traditional Jewish greeting--shalom. However, it would be a mistake to assume that Paul is simply amplifying his Hebraic heritage, as important as that was to him and to the foundations of the Christian faith. In a sense by using "peace" in his greeting, he is saying that all the blessings promised by God to Israel, also belong to the "new Israel of God," the church (Galatians 6:16).

If the Greek greeting needed to be given a religious content, the Hebrew greeting already carried a religious connotation. It seems reasonable that by combining the two greetings that Paul is emphasizing the unity of the church which is made up of both Gentiles and Jews. These people groups who had a history of being hostile to one another have been brought together and form a new creation through our Lord Jesus Christ.

Not quite one-half of the occurrences of the word peace in the New Testament is found in the Pauline writings: 44 out of 93. It is thus an important word in the Pauline vocabulary. Paul uses the word peace in all of his greetings along with the word grace. It is possible, but not certain that this combination of grace and peace in the greeting originated with Paul. The two words are also used together in the greetings of 1 and 2 Peter, 2 and 3 John, and Revelations.

It has often been noted that the result of grace is peace with God. The benefit of receiving and accepting God's great gift so freely given through Jesus Christ, is more than salvation, understood in the limited sense of forgiveness of sins. No, forgiveness is important and wonderful, but peace conveys a much more dynamic and broader notion of being equipped to live in the presence of God, to the glory of God, and as a servant of God.

The Greek term *eirene* (peace), has little content to it outside of quietness, freedom from conflict, etc. The Hebrew term *shalom* developed a meaning of not only peace, but wholeness and well-being, success, happiness, health and all that makes for a satisfying and good life. To state it another way, the Greeks tended to think of peace as a negative, i.e., the absence of wind on a sunny day, the absence of conflict, etc., whereas the Hebrew thought of peace as a positive, i.e., the presence of health, success, etc. Although the Greek concept of peace has no religious connotations attached to it, the concept of shalom in the Old Testament has deep religious roots. It is God, the Creator and Deliverer who gives all that peace implies to the Hebrew mind.

In the Pauline writings God is referred to as the God of peace 6 times (Romans 15:33, 16:20; 2 Corinthians 13:11; Philippians 4:9; 1 Thessalonians 5:23; and 2 Thessalonians 3:16 --"Lord of peace"). Peace as a reference to salvation is mentioned 10 times (Romans 2:10, 5:1, 8:6, 14:17, 15:13; Galatians. 5:22; Ephesians 2:14, 17, 6:15; Colossians 1:20 ("to make peace"). It is used in a relational sense, i.e., to be at peace with others, 13 times (Romans 3:17 [Isaiah 59:8], 14:17, 19; 1 Corinthians 7:15, 14:33 [="order"], 16:11; Galatians. 5:22; Ephesians 2:14, 15, 17; 4:3; Colossians 3:15; 2 Timothy 2:22). And in the sense of a blessing given in 1 Corinthians 16:11, Galatians 6:16; Ephesians 6:23, which are benedictory blessings, plus each of the salutations.

A good example of peace used as a word for salvation is found in Romans 5. Here Paul sounds the note of grace experienced as peace when he wrote,

> *Since we have been justified by faith we have peace with God through our Lord Jesus Christ, through whom we have gained access by faith into this grace in which we now stand. And we rejoice in the hope of the glory of God. Not only so, but we rejoice in our sufferings...because God has poured out his love into our hearts by the Holy Spirit, whom he has given us. (Romans 5:1-5).*

In this passage salvation is described as our having peace with God as result of our being justified by faith. This peace is ours through our Lord

Jesus Christ (cf. also Gal. 1:3-4).

When one considers how the Apostle Paul talks about salvation, probably the first thing that strikes one is that he seldom speaks of the process through which we experience salvation. He does not mention being convicted of one's sins, and only refers to repentance in a salvation context one time (Romans 2:20). He refers to the forgiveness of sins only 7 times, 2 of which are quotations from the Old Testament (Romans 4:7 = Psalms 32:1; 11:27 = Jeremiah 31:34; Ephesians 1:7; 4:32; Colossians 1:14; 2:13; 3:13). The only references to forgiveness which are not quotations from the Old Testament are found in two letters, Ephesians and Colossians.

Rather than writing about the process through which one receives salvation Paul tends to focus on the positive end results of salvation. The primary concepts which Paul uses to describe the conversion experience are: salvation, justified, peace, reconciliation, life, eternal life, freedom and liberation, and new creation.

James D. G. Dunn in his *The Theology of Paul the Apostle,* has a section entitled "Metaphors of Salvation."[63] He arranges the more than 37 metaphors Paul uses under 6 categories: metaphors drawn from 1) the customs of his time; 2) everyday life; 3) agriculture; 4) commerce; 5) religion; and 6) the major events of life. Dunn then goes on to make some insightful observations.

> "Two lines of reflection emerge from consideration of such a kaleidoscope of images. One is that these metaphors bring out the *reality* of the experience of the new beginning for Paul. Evidently they all describe something in the experience of his readers with which they could identify. Something had happened in their lives, something of major importance. Underlying all these metaphors was some tremendously significant event, a turning point of great moment. One does not use images like birth, marriage, and death for everyday occurrences. They only function as images for events which are literally life-changing.
>
> This has a corollary worthy of some attention. For it means that many of Paul's first readers experienced the gospel as acceptance, liberation, or rescue, as cleansing and new dedication, as a dying to an

old life and beginning of a new. There is little evidence that Paul preached for conviction of sin or to stir up feelings of guilt. Nevertheless, for so many of his converts the gospel was received and experienced as an answer to unresolved riddles, as a solution to their plight. In a word, Paul's gospel met real and felt needs

Second, the very different metaphors Paul drew upon were presumably attempts to express as fully as possible a reality which defied a simple or uniform or unifaceted description. There was something so rich and real in the various experiences of conversion which Paul's gospel brought about that Paul had to ransack the language available to him to find ways of describing them. The vitality of the experience made new metaphors necessary if the experience was to be expressed in words (as adequately as that is possible) and to be communicated to others.

This in turn points up another corollary of some interest. For the wide variety of metaphors presumably reflects a wide variety of experiences. Given that variety, it would be a mistake to take any one of Paul's metaphors and to exalt it into some primary or normative status so that all the others must be fitted into its mould. Something like this has happened with the metaphor of justification in classic Protestant theology. In popular evangelism it has happened with the metaphors of salvation and new birth. In such cases there is an obvious danger. The danger is that the event of new beginning in faith comes to be conceptualized as of necessity following a particular pattern, the same for everyone. Equally dangerous is the assumption often made that the same language or imagery must always be used, that experience of individuals must conform to the language which describes it. Instead of diversity of experience and imagery there can be pressure to reduplicate both pattern and jargon, in effect to mass reproduce believers according to a standard formula. Not so with Paul. For him the crucial transition was a many-sided event, and not necessarily the same for any two people..."

Of the metaphors which Paul uses, peace is the most comprehensive. Because of his Jewish background and the all encompassing connotations of the word "peace", it was natural for Paul to use this word, connected with "grace", to convey the new understanding of salvation.

There is, however, another compelling reason why this word "peace" was so appropriate. Faith in Jesus Christ not only changed one's relationship with God, it also effected one's relationships with other believers. Christianity has never been an individualistic religion. Believers are bound to one another to form the body of Christ through which our Lord continues his redemptive ministry to the world. So Paul instructs believers *Make every effort to keep the unity of the Spirit through the bond of peace* (Ephesians 4:3).

In a sermon to the Covenant Midwinter Conference in 1999, John Weborg, professor of Systematic Theology at North Park Theological Seminary, said:

> "A very distinguished Rabbi in Chicago is an acquaintance of mine. I go to him sometimes when I want an interpretation from the inside an Old Testament text. He himself is a survivor of the holocaust. I asked him about shalom, and he said, "Well, peace, yes -- no, but be very careful. Because peace is not the first meaning. The first meaning is that there is shalom if everything fits where it was intended to be. But when anything is out of joint…because of discrimination, because of anti-Semitism, because of the belittling of anything about one's person, there is no shalom, because those don't fit." He went on to say, "The problem with rendering shalom - peace - at least initially is, people jump to the conclusion that if there is no conflict everything is at peace, and thus peace is passive, not active. So you can have all the appearances of peace with the absence of conflict but the condition of shalom is absent because things don't fit."

Jesus gave a new commandment to his followers: *Love one another. As I have loved you, so you must love one another. All men will know that you are my disciples if you love one another* (John 13:34-35). Love demands that we abolish everything in our behavior that does not fit in the life of one who is a Christ follower. The book of Acts indicates that this became a Herculean challenge with the successful mission to the non-Jewish world. Was it possible for Jews and Gentiles, who had deep mistrust and animosity toward each other, to really form one body and work together with a sense of equality and purpose? Paul writes *For [Jesus Christ] himself is our peace, who has made the two one and has destroyed the barrier, the dividing wall of hostility, by abolishing in his flesh the law with its commandments and regulations. His purpose was to create in himself one new man out of the two, thus making peace, and in this one body to reconcile both of them to God through the cross, by which he put to death their hostility...For through him we both have access to the Father by one Spirit* (Ephesians 13-18).

The oneness of the church, the fact that believer's, regardless of their ethnic origins, economic, or cultural differences, are bound together to serve their Lord, Jesus Christ, explains why Paul emphasizes so much that Christians must work and live together in harmony. One of the effects of the sin of pride is that it undermines our relationships with others, especially those who are different from us. As Cornelius Plantinga, Jr. observes: "sin is the vandalism of shalom." [64]

Grace to you and peace summed up the new reality in which those who belong to Christ Jesus live. Because of God's initiative they have salvation as a gift which has changed their relationship to both God and one another. Truly, we are a new creation!

PRAYER PRINCIPLE # 11

Because of Jesus Christ we have a new understanding of salvation.

C. S. Lewis is said to have observed that grace is what distinguishes Christianity from all other world religions. How does your understanding of grace shape your prayers. Does the reality of grace make you more smug or more humble? Why?

Why is peace such an illusive quality in our world? What does not fit in your own life and so destroys or at least makes the experience of peace less dynamic?

A NEW UNDERSTANDING OF GOD

If we were not so familiar with the letters of Paul, the salutations with their designation of God as Father would be shocking to us. Although there is evidence that God was referred to in the synagogue worship as "our Father," it is a designation without much content. With Jesus, however, a whole new perspective is given. "Father" assumes a very personal tone and becomes another name for God. Jesus' use of "Abba" to refer to God (Mark 14:36) introduced an intimacy of relationship with God that is unknown previously and was offensive to much of Jewish piety. The outburst of the opponents of Jesus that he is guilty of blasphemy because he called himself the Son of God (John 10:31-33, 36; Matthew 26:65), shows how far Jesus' use of the term Father to refer to God differed in meaning from that which might possibly have been used in the synagogue. God is referred to as Father in every New Testament book except 3 John, and these references to Father give the impression of being a normal way for the followers of Jesus to refer to God. It is thus clear that the early Christians lived with a new understanding of God because of Jesus.

The Apostle Paul refers to God as Father 42 times. It is important to realize that with the possible exception of Ephesians 3:14, references to God as Father are always connected and anchored with reference to Jesus Christ. Thus God is the God and Father of our Lord Jesus Christ (Romans 15:6; 2 Corinthians 1:3; 11:31; Ephesians 1:3; Colossians 1:3). The coming of Jesus Christ, whom the early Christians recognized as "the Son of God," forever determined and shaped how they thought about God. The eternal, majestic, creator God is brought close in the person of His Son. Although Paul's usual designation for God is *theos - God* - (he uses this term over 500 times) rather than *pater* - Father (used 42 times), nevertheless even in passages where there is no reference to "Father," the concept of God is still influenced by the new understanding that came because of Jesus Christ, God's Son. It is rather fascinating to discover that Paul never refers to Jesus as the Son of the Father, but rather as "the Son of God," and that the Father is referred to as the Father of the *kurios* - Lord. The usage of John is different and Father and Son are often put in juxtaposition to one another.

When we consider the settings in which Paul uses "Father" of God, we discover that this is most often done in a prayer setting. Of the 42 times Paul uses the word "Father" of God, 34 are in the context of a prayer. It would seem that with this word "Father" we enter into an atmosphere of prayer, and that it is especially a vital part of Paul's prayer language. It is also interesting to observe that again and again the reference to God as Father elicits special praise from Paul (2 Corinthians 1:3; 11:31; Galatians 1:4; Ephesians 1:3; 5:20; Philippians 2:11). This may have been due to Paul's Jewish background and the prayers of the Amidah or Eighteen Benedictions.[65]

Father has become a special term to define God. Although there are many metaphors used of God -- Father of mercies, God of all comfort, God of peace, God of hope, to name just a few -- Father stands alone in terms of its significance. Father is not just a metaphorical picture of some action or facet of God's character. It describes something essential for Paul's understanding of God. Paul's encounter with Christ on the road to Damascus and his continuing experience and understanding of Jesus Christ also forced a new understanding of God. Because Jesus is understood by Paul and all of the early Christians as being the Son of God, the one through whom the salvation-will of God has been executed, the understanding of God also experienced a major shift. In Romans 8:31-39 we have a great expression of who God is: *If God be for us who can be against us. He who spared not his own Son but gave him up for us all, will he not also give us all things in him?... Who shall bring any charge against those whom God has chosen?...nothing in all creation can separate us from the love God in Christ Jesus our Lord.* God is not the angry God or the untouchable one, or the distant God-- nor is he only the God of the nation of Israel, or the Creator. In Christ Jesus God has come close and because of Jesus we know that God is love and that his love reaches to us. For the Christian, God is defined by his Son and what he did through and in Christ to bring us salvation. Thus in Paul's most severe letter, Galatians, which is unique because it does not have a reference to his thanking God for them, Paul began: *Paul an apostle--not from men or through men, but through Jesus Christ and God the Father, who raised him from the dead...Grace and peace to you from God our Father and the Lord Jesus Christ, who gave himself for our sins to rescue us from the present evil age, according to the will of our God and Father, to whom be glory for ever and ever. Amen* (Gal. 1:1,3-5). I have underlined the words that show that what Jesus did and accomplished was *according to the will of our*

God and Father. Salvation comes to us through Jesus Christ according to the will of God. It is interesting to note that although Paul can express wonder and appreciation at what Christ has done, this doxological statement and every other one in his writings, (with the exception of 2 Timothy 3:18 which is in praise of Christ) is in response to and in praise to God, sometimes with the designation Father included.

God is not only God the Father, he is also our Father. Through Jesus Christ our relation to God has been changed and there is introduced a new element of intimacy and joy in the Father's presence. Paul's statement in Ephesians 2:18 highlights the special joyful privilege which we enjoy because God in his love redeemed us through Jesus Christ, *Through him we each have access to the Father through the Spirit.* What a privilege, we have access to the eternal, almighty God!

Although the salutations are from both God the Father and the Lord Jesus Christ, God the Father is still seen as having the priority. There can be little doubt that Paul regarded Jesus as fully divine, the image of the invisible God, the One through whom God reveals himself, nevertheless, Paul is careful to point out that ultimately the Father stands alone in his majesty. So we have the statement in 1 Corinthians 15:27-28: *For he 'has put all things under his feet.' (Ps. 8:6) Now when it says that 'everything' has been put under him, it is clear that this does not include God himself, who put everything under Christ. When he has done this, then the Son himself will be made subject to him who put everything under him, so that God may be all in all.* I do not pretend to understand all that this means, but one thing is clear: God the Father stands alone in his majesty and glory.

This is not some isolated text but is evident when one reads texts that praise Christ, such as Philippians 2:5-11 which ends: *every knee shall bow…and every tongue confess that Jesus Christ is Lord, to the glory of God the Father.* These and similar statements are in line with Jesus' own words in John 17:28: *My Father is greater than I* and the many other statements in the Gospels which indicate Jesus' honor and obedience to his Father. Whenever we bow before our Lord Jesus Christ, honor and serve him, this glorifies the Father. In fact, we might say this makes the Father happy. I like how John Piper begins the first chapter of his book, The Pleasures of God.

> "There is a beautiful phrase in 1 Timothy 1:11 buried beneath the too-familiar surface of Bible buzzwords. Before we dig it up, it sounds like this: "The gospel of the glory of the blessed God." But after we dig it up, it sounds like this: "The good news of the glory of the happy God."
>
> A great part of God's glory is his happiness. It was inconceivable to the apostle Paul that God could be denied infinite joy and still be all-glorious. To be infinitely glorious was to be infinitely happy. He used the phrase, "the glory of the happy God," because it is a glorious thing for God to be as happy as he is. God's glory consists much in the fact that he is happy beyond our wildest imagination….
>
> And this is the *gospel:* "The gospel of the glory of the happy God." It is good news that God is gloriously happy. No one would want to spend eternity with an unhappy God. If God is unhappy then the goal of the gospel is not a happy goal, and that means it would be no gospel at all. But, in fact, Jesus invites us to spend eternity with a happy God when he says, "Enter into the *joy* of your master" (Matthew 25:23). Jesus lived and died that *his* joy--God's joy--might be in us and our joy might be full (John 15:11; 17:13). Therefore the gospel is "the gospel of the glory of the happy God." [66]

To discover new depths in our understanding of our heavenly Father enables us to enter into new realms of joy. The Westminster Confession begins with the question: What is the chief end of man? The answer: "The chief end of man is to glorify God and enjoy him forever." To truly "know God" is to be embarked on the adventure of joy.

As evangelicals we have had a strong Christocentric emphasis and since the Charismatic renewal movement also a strong emphasis on the Spirit. Both a Christ focus and a Spirit emphasis, however, is an inadequate expression of the Gospel. For the whole purpose of redemption and sanctification is to reveal to us the Father, to bring us to God. In a wonderfully provocative book, The Forgotten Father, Thomas Smail has written:

> "The Father is in fact 'forgotten' today in pretty much the same way in which the Spirit was 'forgotten' [forty] years ago. To 'remember' him is not so much to turn our intellectual interest in a new direction, but is much more like the remembering of the Lord's Supper, where we are summoned to an opening of our hearts, a reorientation of our faith, a personal and corporate restoration of our relationship, so that we realize anew with praise and wonder that in Christ we have, not only forgiveness of sins and the gift of the Spirit, but above all access to the Father. When he who has been in that sense 'forgotten' is in that sense 'remembered,' we are once more in the presence of one of these events and actions of the Holy Spirit that mean radical renewal for God's people. It is in that expectation, and in a perspective that is at once theological, practical and personal that we are called to 'know the Father' which, as 1 John 2:13 makes clear, is a defining qualification of those who are his children."[67]

In an age in which so much emphasis is placed on "my experience," it is easy to lose sight of who God is and simply relegate God to "my experience of God." It is significant that in two passages in which Paul emphasizes the Christian's experience of the Spirit who causes us to cry out "Abba, Father", he is not writing about some ecstatic or esoteric experience, but rather of the profound realization that we are indeed children of God (Romans 8:15; Galatians 4:6). The emphasis is upon the truth that we are no longer slaves but have been adopted and are now God's children, which is confirmed by the Holy Spirit. The proper attitude of a child is one of humility and wonder as we discover, or should I say, it is revealed to us through the Spirit, that God is truly "our/my Father," because of Jesus Christ.

"Abba, Father" is a strange expression to found in letters addressed to Romans and Greeks. The only reason that an Aramaic word should find itself inserted into these letters is that this is a common memory of the early Christians of the word which Jesus used in prayer: he addressed God as "Abba, Father." Jesus himself gave his disciples the right to address God as Abba (Luke 11:2). Abba was not just a word of a child that expressed intimacy with the father, but also was a word of deep respect which recognized the authority and honor of the father. The early

Christians evidently valued this word from the lips of Jesus as the expression of the reality of having an intimate and submissively reverent relationship to the Father which affirmed their status as being truly His children through Jesus Christ.

Whenever Paul refers to God as "Father", we should sense the joyful wonder that underlies the expression. Prayer is the proper setting of this emotion, as the very act of praying implies the humble acknowledgement of our dependence on God. As Father, God remains the sovereign, almighty One, but through Jesus Christ he has been revealed as the great lover of his Son and of all who accept God's gift of redemption through him. As we call God, "Father," we become children again, and Jesus said, *I tell you the truth, unless you change and become like little children, you will never enter the kingdom of heaven. Therefore, whoever humbles himself like this child is the greatest in the kingdom of heaven* (Matthew 18:3-4). A child is dependent on the father's care, provision, approval, will, and goodness. Too often we approach God as though he is just like us except he has a higher office with more authority and power. But God is not like us! One of the purposes of redemption is that we might become like Him! The only attitude that is appropriate for one who prays to God the Father, is a humble, submissive reverence that is confident of the Father's love and goodness.

In past generations the spiritual life of God's people was often nurtured on the contemplation of the attributes of God. As one sets out to contemplate and think about God as he is in himself, and guided by the Scriptures, one becomes aware that s/he is being changed into his likeness (2 Corinthians 3:18). Some books that have been helpful to me, besides the older standard works which are sometimes hard to read, are J. I Packer's, Knowing God; John Piper's, Desiring God and The Pleasures of God; and A. W. Tozer's, The Pursuit of the Holy. It matters not whether you are in full agreement with what an author writes, if they help you think more deeply about God and you rely on the Holy Spirit to give you added insight, you will be thrust into that wonderful land of awe, majesty, glory, and holiness. The more you know God, the more interesting he becomes and the greater the mystery and wonder that such a God should love the world, and you personally, so much that he would send his only

Son that whoever believes in him should not perish but have eternal life.

DOXOLOGIES

I think it is appropriate to close this section on God the Father by considering briefly the doxological statements that occur in Paul's letters.

From the beginning of my reading of the letters of Paul as a teenager, I can recall my delight in the way that Paul interrupts what he is writing to express praise to God. These often came to me as somewhat of a surprise. I now realize that this spirit of verbal praise to God is because of Paul's Jewish background where it was normal to bless God many times throughout the day.

One of the things the letters of Paul reveal to us, is that the praise of God seems to have been close to the surface of his consciousness and the praises he gives are sometimes formal and some more informal. Often they are shaped by his background as a Jewish rabbi.

There are sixteen doxological statements and all but one, 2 Timothy 4:18, which is in praise of Christ, have God as the object of the praise. These can be divided into three categories, determined by their form.

Five are statements of praise that is elicited by something Paul has just written. They have the feel of being a spontaneous expression of adoration and praise (Romans 1:25; 9:5; 1 Corinthians 11:31; Galatians 1:5; Philippians 4:20. And possibly Romans 11:36, which comes at the conclusion of a longer doxological statement which is a composite of Old Testament verses). An example of this type is Romans 1:25 which comes after three paragraphs of his describing the rebellion of mankind and the wrath of God: *They exchanged the truth of God for a lie, and worshiped and served created things rather than the Creator--who is forever praised. Amen.* He then continues to describe how God's wrath has been expressed: *God gave them over to shameful lusts.* This short spontaneous praise to God seems to have been drawn from Paul by his abhorrence of the thought that mankind should refuse to worship God the Creator, who is worthy of all praise, and place the creation above the Creator.

Seven precede and introduce a statement which he is about to make which causes him to be especially thankful and express his praise and end with "Amen" (Romans 7:25; 1 Corinthians 15:57; 2 Corinthians 1:3; 2:14; 8:16; 9:15; and Ephesians 1:3). An example of this type is 2 Corinthians

8:16, *I thank God, who put into the heart of Titus the same concern I have for you.* When Paul thought about Titus he expresses a simple *I thank God.* The Ephesians 1:3 praise introduces an extended passage praising God for his grace and purposes. It has often been observed that Ephesians 1:3-14 is almost in the form of a prayer. In fact if one changes the third person pronouns to the second with the appropriate other modifications this would demand, the whole passage could be read as a beautiful prayer of praise.

Three are more formal and liturgical expressions of praise. They are longer and more complex than the other forms and have the feel of something planned and lack the sense of spontaneity. They each conclude with "Amen" (Romans 11:33-36; 1 Timothy 1:17; 6:14-16). An example of this type is 1 Timothy 1:17, *Now to the King eternal, immortal, invisible, the only God, be honor and glory for ever and ever. Amen.* This doxology is drawn from Paul as he thinks about God's mercy and call to him personally, and has the content and terminology which probably only one trained in the rabbinical school would easily use.

The one doxology that is in praise to Christ is interesting as it concludes a moving statement of pathos, disappointment and deliverance:

> *At my first defense, no one came to my support, but everyone deserted me. But the Lord stood at my side and gave me strength, so that through me the message might be fully proclaimed and all the Gentiles might hear it. And I was delivered from the lion's mouth. The Lord will rescue me from every evil and will bring me safely to his heavenly kingdom. To him be glory for ever and ever. Amen (2 Timothy 4:16-18).*

Here in the last letter he wrote before his execution, Paul demonstrates that one can give praise even when things are difficult and the outlook is intensely bleak. His confidence and hope in Christ enables him to look up in a joyful expectation that "the best is yet to be." Although the majority of critical scholars deny Pauline authorship for the Pastoral letters, I find it difficult to believe that anyone but Paul could have written these moving words of faith and praise. For another doxology to Christ see Revelation 1:6.

When one considers these statements of praise one is impressed by the simplicity of most of them. Paul found occasion to simply say "thank you" to God in the midst of his day. At times this would call forth a special word of joyful praise to the God who is so majestic, merciful, kind and compassionate. Because of Paul's adoration of God, praise was a normal part of his life, not something added or put on for the sake of others. The more one has eyes to see the hand of God in their life and world, the more natural are the expressions of praise. Perhaps the prayer of Elisha for his servant in 2 Kings 6:17 should be ours: *O LORD open [my] eyes so [I] may see.*

PRAYER PRINCIPLE # 12

God is our Father

How does the concept of Father impact the way you pray? Are there hurdles you have had to move past in order to meaningfully address God as Father?

In a society in which there has been so much bad and inadequate fathering, what can we and the body of faith do to fill up what is lacking for many?

What are the positive emotions that addressing God as Father brings to you? What is added when we realize that God is the Father of our Lord Jesus Christ?

Write your own doxology in praise of God.

A NEW UNDERSTANDING OF JESUS CHRIST

Each of the salutations is not only from God the Father but also from the Lord Jesus Christ. This is really an amazing thing and reflects the profound conviction of the early church that "Jesus Christ is Lord." This is not some belief that developed over a period of time, but seems to have been a conviction from the earliest time following the resurrection of Jesus. Luke recounts how in Peter's sermon on the Day of Pentecost he had said that *God has made this Jesus, whom you crucified, both Lord and Christ* (Acts 2:36). And the Apostle Paul can write to the Corinthians, *We do not preach ourselves, but Jesus Christ as Lord...* (2 Corinthians 4:5).

Jesus is Lord was probably the earliest of Christian creeds and an essential part of the earliest belief system of the followers of Jesus (cf.

Romans 10:9; 1 Corinthians 12:3; Philippians 2:10). The very fact that Paul can give this blessing from both God the Father and the Lord Jesus Christ indicates that Jesus is regarded as in some sense worthy of worship and praise and the source of blessings along with the Father.

"Lord" and "Christ" were originally titles which quickly became proper names of Jesus. Each of these names can be used alone or in combination, and they can be interchanged without any apparent change in meaning or emphasis. Each of the three names -- Jesus, Christ, Lord -- have had special meaning for Christians down through the ages.

JESUS is the human face of God. Jesus is Immanuel, God with us (Matthew 1:23). He reveals to us what God is like. As Paul notes in 2 Corinthians 4:6, *For God, who said, "Let light shine out of darkness," made his light to shine in our hearts to give us the light of the knowledge of the glory of God in the face of Christ.* And in Colossians 2:9 he writes, *For in Christ all the fullness of the Deity lives in bodily form...* . Jesus is God coming close to walk where we walk, to know our sorrow, and to be God's remedy for our sin. In the cross of Jesus the affects of our disobedience upon God is made visible and the terrible cost to God which his love for us cost him -- *He...did not spare his own Son, but gave him up for us all* (Romans 8:32).

I find it interesting that the Hebrew name for Jesus is *Yohoshua (transliterated = Joshua, Jesus is the Greek equivalent)* and means "the Lord saves" (Matthew 1:21) *Yahweh* is the sacred name for God and was never pronounced but instead the word *Adonai -- Lord* was substituted. What is interesting is that the only thing that differentiates the Hebrew name of Jesus from Yahweh is one letter (YHSHWH --YHWH) and that one letter simply changes the meaning to include the mission of Jesus-- to save us. It is also interesting to note that the Hebrew shin (sh) is a symbol for "the Almighty". Jews place this symbol on their mezuzah and on the tefelin. It is a revelation of the oneness of God as well as the divinity of the Messiah. Thus Jesus is not only LORD, but he is also identified with El Shaddai, "the Almighty" (Genesis 17:1).[68]

Jesus suffered and died for you and for me, and his suffering and death is the proof of how much God cares and loves us. In Jesus we see one who had compassion on the multitudes, patience with his disciples, one who knew temptation and heartache. Jesus reveals to us what God is like. St Bernard of Clairvaux puts it this way:

> "The name of Jesus is both light and nourishment. . . As honey to the taste, as melody in the ear, as songs of gladness in the heart, so is the name of Jesus. And medicine it is as well. . . Naught but the name of Jesus can restrain the impulse of anger, repress the swelling of pride, cure the wound of envy, bridle the onslaught (love) of luxury, extinguish the flame of carnal desire--can temper avarice (greed), and put to flight impure and ignoble thoughts. For when I name the name of Jesus, I call to mind at once a Man meek (gentle) and lowly of heart, benign (kind), pure, temperate, merciful; a Man conspicuous for every honorable and saintly quality; and also in the same Person the Almighty God--so that He both restores me to health by His example and renders me strong by His assistance. No less than this is brought to my mind by the name of Jesus whenever I hear it."[69]

CHRIST: literally means "the anointed one" and is the Greek equivalent to the Jewish word for "Messiah." According to Luke, when Jesus preached his first sermon in Nazareth, he read from the prophecy of Isaiah, chapter 61: *For the Spirit of the Lord is upon me because he has anointed me ...* . Jesus then said that these words were fulfilled in their hearing; i.e., he was the anointed one. In his own person he is the fulfillment of God's promises in the Old Testament to send the Messiah. For the Christian the name Christ reminds us that God can be trusted and always keeps his promises. As Paul states in 2 Corinthians 1:20, *For no matter how many promises God has made, they are "Yes" in Christ...* . And Galatians 4:4 Paul reminds us that when the time is right he will act. *But when the time had fully come, God sent his Son...* . It is good for us to know that we are in his hands and although his ways are not our ways, we can always trust him to do what is best.

LORD: Although the word translated Lord can be used simply as a polite form of address, meaning "Sir" (especially in the Gospels and a few places in Acts), in the letters of the New Testament, except in some quotations from the Old Testament, "Lord" always refers to Jesus. We can be even more specific: "Lord" refers to Jesus as the risen and exalted One. Since "kyrios, LORD" was the common LXX (Septuagint) translation for "Yahweh," it is difficult to imagine that the earliest Christians had not made a connection of the man Jesus with the revelation of God's name to Moses and the worship of the LORD in the Old Testament. There is no evidence in the New Testament that there was an uneasiness with this designation of Jesus as "kyrios, Lord" and it is hard to escape the overtones that this designation was also the acknowledgement of the divinity of Jesus.

That the Apostle Paul could write: *For God, who said, 'Let light shine out of darkness,' made his light to shine in our hearts to give us the light of the knowledge of the glory of God in the face of Christ* (2 Corinthians 4:6), indicates an extremely high view of Jesus.

The belief is that Jesus is essential for salvation, so Paul can write in Romans 10:9, *If you confess with your mouth, "Jesus is Lord," and believe in your heart that God raised him from the dead, you will be saved.* When Jesus is called Lord, the focus is upon the ascended and exalted One, who sits at the right hand of God. It is important to observe, however, that Paul and all the writers of the New Testament make a careful distinction between God and Jesus. It is God who has exalted Jesus and given him the name Lord (Phil. 2:10-11).

It is remarkable that things are attributed to Jesus Christ the Lord which were formerly reserved for God alone.

- He rules over all humanity (Romans 14:9).

- He has intentions for us, so we are told *Do not be foolish but understand what the will of the Lord is* (Ephesians 5:17). He gives insight (2 Timothy 2:7) and visions and revelations (2 Corinthians 12:1)

- He is faithful (2 Thessalonians 3:3) and merciful (2 Timothy 1:16)

- He is the Lord of peace and gives peace (2 Thessalonians 3:16).

- His name is to be glorified (2 Thessalonians 1:12).
- The Old Testament "Day of the Lord" has become a reference to Jesus' second coming (1 Thessalonians 5:2).
- Jesus is the judge before whom we will give an account of our lives (2 Corinthians 5:10; 2 Timothy 4:8). As judge he gives out rewards (Colossians 3:24) and he punishes (1 Thessalonians 4:6).
- The Lord forgives us (Colossians 3:13).
- We are washed, sanctified and justified in the name of the Lord (1 Corinthians 6:11).
- Christ is our righteousness, holiness and redemption (1 Corinthians 1:30).
- Christ is creator (Colossians 1:16; 1 Corinthians 8:6).
- He is our protector and keeper (Ephesians 6:10; 1 Corinthians 15:57).
- He is the image of the invisible God (2 Corinthians 4:6; Colossians 1:15) and in 2 Timothy 4:18 the Apostle can give a doxology to Christ: *The Lord will rescue me from every evil attack and will bring me safely to his heavenly kingdom. To him be glory for ever and ever. Amen.*

There are statements made about God and then with no ambivalence whatsoever, Christ is referred to as providing the same benefits. Perhaps the clearest example of this is 1 Corinthians 8:6, *yet for us there is but one God, the Father, from whom all things came and for whom we live; and there is but one Lord, Jesus Christ, through whom all things came and through whom we live.*

All of these designations (and more, plus the references related to Jesus as the Head of the Church) are given to Christ without in any way diminishing the praise and worship of God. In fact the exaltation and praise of the Lord Jesus Christ brings glory and delight to God the Father. For it is God who has exalted Jesus and given him a name above all other names so that *at the name of Jesus every knee shall bow...and every tongue confess that Jesus Christ is Lord to the glory of God the Father* (Philippians 2:10-11).

The Mystery of God

With the confession that Jesus Christ is Lord we are ushered into the mystery of God. That Paul could write *Grace to you and peace from God our Father AND the Lord Jesus Christ,* is extraordinary. The very heart of biblical faith is stated in Deuteronomy 6:4 and affirmed and quoted by Jesus in Mark 12:29; *Hear, O Israel, the Lord our God, the Lord is one.* For Paul to list the blessing as coming from both God the Father and the Lord Jesus Christ indicates that something has occurred that both changes and enriches the understanding of God. Without any change in belief as to the oneness of God, Jesus Christ the Lord is elevated to the position of divinity.

Paul in Colossians 2:2 wrote, *My purpose is that they may be encouraged in heart and united in love, so that they may have complete understanding, in order that they may know the mystery of God, namely Christ, in whom are hidden all the treasures of wisdom and knowledge.* Christ is the door to understanding the mystery of God. As Jesus Christ is elevated and recognized as Lord, we are introduced to the first stages of the development of the doctrine of the Trinity. Although God is One, there is a threeness in the oneness. There is no evidence that the early Christians were uneasy with this radical change in their belief about God. The acknowledgement that "God was in Christ" and that Christ revealed God was the result of their experience of God, not of theoretical speculation. The exaltation of Jesus as Lord did not in any way threaten the adoration and worship of the Father. Rather it enriched it. The Father always has priority as 1 Corinthians 15:27-28 bears witness. The mystery of God is that he is greater and more complex and more interesting than had been realized before. Christ becomes the key to the understanding of God. The more one understands of Jesus Christ the more that is revealed about God, for in Christ are hidden all the treasures of wisdom and knowledge.

To refer to Jesus as "Lord" is to acknowledge that he is Master and Owner and is to be worshipped, honored, praised and obeyed along with God the Father.

PRAYER PRINCIPLE # 13

Jesus is Lord

The author believes that the confession, "Jesus is Lord," involves an affirmation of the deity of Jesus. Do you agree? Why, or why not?

What is the difference between believing Jesus is Lord and inviting him to be Lord of your life?

The following prayer comes from Peter Horrobin in a lecture I heard him give. If you find it meaningful, pray it aloud for yourself.

"Thank you Jesus for dying on the cross for my sins. I confess that I am a sinner in need of a Savior; and today, Jesus, I want to invite you to be the Lord of every area of my life,

I invite you to be the Lord of my mind and all my thinking;
Lord of my emotions and all my reactions;
Lord of my will and all my decisions;
Lord of my body and all my behavior;
Lord of my sexuality and all its expressions;
Lord of my finances and all my earning and spending;
Lord of my spirit and my relationship with God;
And Lord of my destiny and my future.
I invite you, Jesus, to come and reign in my life. Amen."

What areas of your life do you find it most difficult to submit to Christ's Lordship?

A NEW UNDERSTANDING OF OURSELVES: WE ARE SERVANTS

It should not come as a surprise that because the gospel gives us a new understanding of salvation, God and Jesus, that it also changes how we think of ourselves. Although this is not explicitly stated in the greetings, it is certainly implied. We are no longer just sinners who are estranged from God, we are sinners redeemed through the blood of Christ and made a new creation. Paul can even write that because of the great

exchange -- Christ became what we are in order that we might become what he is -- we are the righteousness of God in Christ: *God made him who had no sin to be sin for us, so that in him we might become the righteousness of God*
(2 Corinthians 5:21).

Paul uses a number of word pictures to describe our new status. A few of them are: we are a new creation; we are reconciled to God; we are saved; we are adopted and now are God's children; we are ambassadors for Christ; and we are fellow heirs with Christ. As we begin to understand our new identity in Christ it will effect our behavior and values and we seek to *redeem the time, because the days are evil* (Ephesians 5:17).

If Jesus is truly Lord and we seek to worship and serve him, we must recognize that we are called to be his servants. *You are not your own; you were bought at a price. Therefore honor God with your body*
(1 Corinthians 6:19-20). This understanding lies at the heart of Paul's ethical teaching.

Paul states this of himself. *Paul a servant of Christ Jesus (Romans 1:1) Paul and Timothy, servants of Christ Jesus* (Philippians 1:1). Both James (1:1) and Peter (2 Peter 1:1) refer to themselves as servants of Jesus Christ. There is often an evident sense of wonder when Paul writes about the privilege and responsibility that God has given him when he called him and entrusted to him the ministry of the gospel Christ.

We, who are followers of Jesus, are also servants of the Lord. There are only three explicit statements that we serve the Lord in Paul's writings: *Be devoted to one another in brotherly love. Honor one another above yourselves. Never be lacking in zeal, but keep your spiritual fervor, serving the Lord.* (Romans 12:10-11), and two references in instructions to slaves: *Slaves, obey your earthly masters with respect and fear, and with sincerity of heart, just as you would obey Christ. Obey them…like slaves of Christ, doing the will of God from your heart. Serve wholeheartedly, as if you were serving the Lord, not men, because you know that the Lord will reward everyone for whatever good he does…* (Ephesians 6:5-8). *Whatever you do, work at it with all your heart, as working for the Lord, not men, since you know that you will receive an inheritance from the Lord as a reward. It is the Lord Christ you are serving* (Colossians 3:23-

24). Although these are the only explicit references in Paul's writings to the Christian being a servant of the Lord, it is implied over and over again. Not the least of the allusions to our being the Lord's servants is the theme that the Church is the body of Christ.

In the Old Testament to be called a servant of the Lord was a very honored title. It is applied to special people including Abraham, Moses, David, the prophets, the people of Israel, and in Isaiah 40-55 it is applied to the suffering servant.

William Barclay summarizes what the title "servant of Christ" meant to Paul:

> "Paul claims to be a servant (*doulos*) of Christ. *Doulos* is more than a *servant*; it is *slave.* A servant is free to come and go, and to attach himself to another master; but a slave is the possession of his master for ever. When Paul calls himself the slave of Jesus Christ, he does three things. (i) He lays down that he is the absolute possession of Christ. Christ loved him, and Christ has bought him with a price (1 Cor. 6:20), and he can never belong to anyone but Christ. (ii) He lays it down that he owes an absolute obedience to Christ. The slave has no will of his own; his master's will must be his will, and his master's decision must regulate his life. So Paul has no will but the will of Christ, and no obedience but to his savior and Lord. (iii) In the OT the regular title of the prophets is *the servants of God* (Amos 3:7; Jere. 7:25). The title is given to Moses, to Joshua, and to David (Joshua 1:2; Judges 2:8; Ps. 78:70; 89:3, 10). In point of fact, the highest of all titles of honor is *servant of God*; and when Paul takes this title, he humbly places himself in the succession of the prophets, and of the great ones of God. The Christian's slavery to Jesus Christ is no cringing and abject subjection… 'To be His slave is to be a king.' To be the slave of Christ is the way to perfect freedom." [70]

The essential characteristics of the servant of the Lord, which is true of all ages, is set forth in Isaiah 42:1-4:[71] These verses are quoted by Matthew in 12:18-21 as an explanation of why Jesus did what he did. At the baptism of Jesus and also at the transfiguration the voice from heaven speaks words that are drawn from Isaiah 42:1 and Psalm 2:7, and as such they define for Jesus what his role is to be. Thus Isaiah 42:1-4 was important for Jesus' understanding of his mission. Isaiah 42:1-4 reads:

> *Here is my servant, whom I uphold, my chosen one in whom I delight; I will put my Spirit on him and he will bring justice to the nations. He will not shout or cry out, or raise his voice in the streets. A bruised reed he will not break, and a smoldering wick he will not snuff out. In faithfulness he will bring forth justice; he will not falter or be discouraged till he establishes justice on earth, In his law the islands will put their hope.*

While this has primary reference to Jesus Christ, THE servant, it also applies to all God's servants. Note the following four characteristics of the servant of the Lord drawn from Isaiah 42:1-4.

1. The servant is chosen by God.

Here is my servant, whom I uphold, my chosen one in whom I delight… . Isaiah 42:1.

We evangelicals place a strong emphasis on the necessity of having a personal relationship with Christ by accepting Christ and making a decision to follow Jesus. A person's response to Christ is fundamentally important. However, we must never forget that we are *responding* to Christ's call to us. In the scriptures it is always God who takes the initiative. I have often thought of the story in Genesis 3 as the basic paradigm of the whole Bible. For the Bible is not the story of mankind's search for God, but rather of God's search for mankind. In the story in Genesis 3 it tells how the Lord God would come down in the evening to walk and have fellowship with the man and woman. After they had eaten the forbidden fruit, we are told that their eyes were opened and they were ashamed because they were naked. When the Lord came down to walk with them they hid themselves. And God called out "Adam, Where are you?" That is not the cry of an angry God but of a broken hearted Father who knows that his children have disobeyed him. The rest of the Bible is the account of God seeking mankind. When Jesus needed to respond to the criticism of his eating with sinners and tax collectors, in Luke 15 he tells three stories: A shepherd who hunts for a lost sheep, a woman who hunts for a lost coin, and a father who has a son go off into the far country, but who welcomes the wayward son home again. In telling those stories, Jesus is saying that he is only doing what God has always done, seek the lost. God is constantly seeking the rebellious sinful person. We could not accept him if he did not open our eyes to our need and move our hearts by his Spirit.

There is an old hymn written by an unknown author that beautifully expresses this.

"I sought the Lord, and afterward I knew He moved my soul to seek him, seeking me;

It was not I that found, O Savior true: No I was found of thee.

I find, I walk, I love, but O the whole of love is but my answer, Lord, to thee; For thou wert long before-hand with my soul: Always thou lovedst me."[72]

In the Gospel of John, Jesus tells his disciples: *You did not chose me, but I chose you to go and bear fruit--fruit that will last* (John 15:16). Oswald Chambers comment is right on the mark:

" *'I have chosen you.'* That is the way the grace of God begins. It is a constraint we cannot get away from; We can disobey it, but we cannot generate it. The drawing is done by the supernatural grace of God, and we never can trace where His work begins."[73]

I resonate to what Michael Casey wrote in *Towards God,*

> "There is a providence of God active in the life of every person. This is no blueprint which once settled cannot be changed. It is a patient, paternal, infinitely loving willingness to provide a way from wherever we are to our Father's house. If we are off course or going backward or completely stationary, a way can still be plotted. There is always a way. To put ourselves outside the providence of God would be like falling off the edge of the earth. It can't happen, because if we go far enough in the wrong direction we end up within easy distance of where we should be. Strangely, in letting us wander off on our own, God often creates through different means the very virtues we rejected in choosing our own way. It would be wrong to imagine God as resentful or sullen about having to keep updating our routes back. In fact, I would not be surprised if the challenge of ensnaring particularly rebellious human wills appealed to the Creator's sense of play… .[74]

A servant realizes that his/her service is simply a response of love to the one who loved and called them and who gave himself up for them (Galatians 2:20).

Paul in his wonderful pageant of praise in Ephesians 1:4-6 speaks of God choosing us in Christ *"before the creation of the world to be holy and blameless in his sight. In love he predestined us to be adopted as his [children] through Jesus Christ, in accordance with his pleasure and will--to the praise of his glorious grace, which he has freely given us in the One he loves." (cf. 2 Thessalonians 2:13).* There is a sense that when God chose to enter into our humanity in the person of his Son Jesus Christ, he is saying to us, "I refuse to be God apart from you." In Jesus Christ, God has so bound himself to his human creation, that men and women, boys and girls have also become the inhabits of God's heaven. Jesus said: *If I go and prepare a place for you, I will come back and take you to be with me that you also may be where I am* (John 14:3).

To be a servant means that we submit ourselves and all we are and have to the Lord for his use. Our lives are no longer our own (cf. Galatians 2:20; 1 Corinthians 6:19-20; Romans 6:13) but are to be lived for the glory of God and the service of our Lord, Jesus Christ. One of the themes that runs through the prayers of the Apostle Paul is that we might live lives worthy of our calling (Colossians 1;10; Ephesians 1:18).

PRAYER PRINCIPLE # 14

We are Servants of God and chosen by him

In what way does the concept of having been chosen by God effect how you think of yourself? How you act? and thus how you pray?

The life of a servant is marked by submission and obedience. Share a time when you were able to fully submit your will to God. How did you feel? What was the result of this obedience?

2. The servant of the Lord is marked by the presence of the Holy Spirit.

Here is my servant...I will put my Spirit upon him. (Isaiah 42:1)

One cannot be a servant of the Lord unless he has given to us the Holy Spirit. This is why Jesus commanded the disciples to stay in Jerusalem until they received the Holy Spirit (Luke 24:49). The presence of the Holy Spirit is the quintessential quality of a servant of the Lord as Paul emphasized when he wrote: *If anyone does not have the Spirit of Christ he does not belong to Christ* (Romans 8:9). One of the great differences between the Old Testament and the New Testament is that in the Old Testament the Spirit is given to a person, somewhat like a work uniform, which is taken off when the work is done. The Spirit comes upon a person to enable them to do what God has called them to do and then this special presence of God is withdrawn. Jesus Christ is the first person in history in which the Spirit came and remained. This is emphasized by the Gospel of John in several ways. I will mention only two. John the Baptist testified that God had informed him: *He on whom you see the Spirit descend and remain, this is he who baptizes with the Holy Spirit* (John 1:33). And Jesus, preparing the disciples for his departure and their continuing ministry said: *I will pray the Father and he will give you another Counselor, to be with you for ever, even the Spirit of truth, whom the world cannot receive, because it neither sees him nor knows him; you know him, for he dwells with you, and will be in you* (John 14:16-17 emphasis added). Jesus knew the experiential reality of the empowering presence of the Holy Spirit, and he gave this same Spirit to the disciples on the Day of Pentecost. The same Holy Spirit who empowered Jesus dwells and empowers the Christian today.

But what does it look and feel like to be filled with the Spirit of God? Does it make us strange, other worldly, misfits in this world? Rudolf Schlatter, a German Biblical scholar, notes that through their fellowship with Jesus the disciples learned "that their personal consciousness, so far from being suspended by the operation of the Spirit, was actually sanctified and perfected…Jesus is always content to remain a member of the natural community; he does not regard his involvement in the natural order as an infringement of his status as the Son of God. Hence his service to God always takes the form of establishing fellowship with men. In him whom they adored as the perfect work and bearer of the Spirit, the disciples had a standard by which to judge the working of the Spirit in themselves and in the Church. Thus their conception of the Spirit was controlled by the knowledge of God which proceeded from their communion with Jesus. Here was no occasional, piecemeal meeting with God, which was all that mantic piety could offer, but a gift of God which gave a unity to their lives."[75]

The Holy Spirit, too often, is regard as an added ingredient to the Christian life. But the truth of the matter is that all authentic Christian experience is experience of the Holy Spirit. When Jesus told Nicodemus that he must be "born again," he defined this as being "born of the Spirit" (John 3:8). While there are certainly extraordinary gifts of the Spirit, I am struck by the fact that most of the gifts are really quite ordinary and seem to involve the heightening of natural skills and inclinations so that we are more effective and are able to enrich others to the glory of God (see the gifts listed in Romans 12:6-8; 1 Corinthians 12:7-11; 27-31).

As Christians, we are to be continuously under the control of the empowering presence of the Holy Spirit (Ephesians 5:18). As we live by the Spirit we are able to put aside the things that displease God and this enables the Spirit to cause his fruit, which produces Christlikeness, to flourish in our lives (Galatians 5:7-24). James D. G. Dunn, in his book <u>*Jesus and the Spirit*</u>, observes that "*when Paul wants to find the distinctive mark of Spirit-given experience, he finds it not in the charismatic Spirit as such, nor in the eschatological Spirit as such, but in the Jesus Spirit, the Spirit whose characteristics are those of Christ;* he experiences the Spirit as a power which owns the Lordship of Jesus, which reproduces for the believer Jesus' relationship of sonship with the Father, which creates the believer's character afresh after the pattern of Christ…In Paul then *the distinctive mark of the Spirit becomes his Christness.*"[76] It would not be incorrect then to say that the most distinctive characteristic of the Holy Spirit in the New Testament is his Jesus quality, and Paul states that God's intention and will for us is that we would be "conformed to the image of his Son" (Romans 8:29). This is being accomplished as we focus on the Lord Jesus Christ, for *we…are being transformed into his likeness with ever-increasing glory, which comes from the Lord, who is the Spirit*
(2 Corinthians 3:18).

The issue for the Christian is not "How can I receive the Holy Spirit?", but rather "How can I appropriate the power of the Spirit so that it is a transforming reality in my life?" The answer to this question is so simple that we tend to reject it. We appropriate the Holy Spirit by sincerely worshipping the Triune God (both privately and corporately) and consciously seeking to live in the presence of God and please him more and more. This means that we seek to be obedient to what we understand to be God's will for us at this time and in this place. It is not so much a matter of technique or our doing something. It is a matter of who we are, of intention and Being.

Recently I have done some reading in Greek Orthodox spirituality and came across some thoughts by Gregory Collins OSB to which I found myself resonating:

> "By faith we understand that although we may talk about placing ourselves in the presence of God, this is in fact inaccurate. The Trinity is perpetually present to us: it is we who are absent from God. We are often spiritually anaesthetized, immersed in a sea of forgetfulness, oblivious to the light of the divine energies, despite the fact that they are continually shining upon us.
>
> When we awaken from this spiritual sleep we need to identify how God is present to us, and find some way, some simple 'method' to help us maintain our awareness of him. Prayer means concentration and expansion: concentrating on the presence of God, and at the same time allowing him to expand our consciousness towards infinity.
>
> How is God present to us? He is of course present as the One who upholds the world at every point by his creative word…But Eastern Christian writers and mystics insist that this kind of presence is only the beginning. There is a deeper realization of God's presence available to us. Through the coming of Christ and the Holy Spirit, God wishes to dwell within us in a new way: not in a mode of which we are largely unconscious, or as a kind of spiritual atmosphere in which we simply live and move and have our being (Acts 17:28), but as a lover and friend (Song of Solomon 5:10). God wants his presence to be consciously experienced by us…
>
> The 'place' where God manifests his presence is the heart, the

temple of the self. It is the location of the inner senses where the deepest roots of one's interiority lie, where the light of consciousness emerges out of the thick darkness of insensibility. Here in this metaphysical matrix of the personality body and soul are one in a unity greater than any dualism. Here too, the deepest unity between God and human beings is grounded. This is the temple, the meeting place between God and human beings, into which he pours his Spirit…

Orthodox writers like to describe the spiritual life as the descent of the mind into the heart. The thinking, logical, superficial intelligence symbolically associated with the head, and related to the 'outer' world by sense perception, must be baptized into a kind of inner death and resurrection. Vision must return from distracting dissipation to inner concentration. Just as Christ died, descended into the underworld and rose again, so we must die to the limited understanding of the mind and senses, by descending into this deep interiority through prayer. In the cavern of the heart we will meet the indwelling Christ. We will know an inner Easter and an interior Pentecost in the power of the Holy Spirit who is given to those who follow the descent of Christ."[77]

It is interesting how many writers of spirituality urge us to live from the heart, from the center of our being, where we will find the presence of God. Our lives are so busy and noisy that we often live as practical atheists. One of the great purposes of prayer is to help us remember and thus open ourselves to God who dwells within us through the Holy Spirit. One of the fascinating things to discover is that when we are in touch with God at a deep level, we are also drawn outward to other people, to the world that God loves. Henri Nouwen has an interesting description of the necessity and importance of living from the center, the heart:

"I have always been fascinated by those wagon wheels: with their wide rims, strong wooden spokes and big hubs. These wheels help me to understand the importance of a life lived from the center. When I move along the rim, I can reach one spoke after the other, but when I stay at the hub, I am in touch with all the spokes at once.

To pray is to move to the center of all life and all love. The closer I come to the hub of life, the closer I come to all that receives its strength and energy from there. My tendency is to get so distracted by the diversity of the many spokes of life that I am busy but not truly life-giving, all over the place but not focused. By directing my attention to the heart of life, I am connected with its rich variety while remaining centered. What does the hub represent? I think of it as my own heart, the heart of God, and the heart of the world. When I pray, I enter into the depth of my own heart and find there the heart of God, who speaks to me of love. I recognize, right there, the place where all my sisters and brothers are in communion with one another. The great paradox of the spiritual life is, indeed, that the most personal is most universal, that the most intimate, is the most communal, and that the most contemplative is most active.

The wagon wheel shows that the hub is the center of all energy and movement, even when it often seems not to be moving at all. In God all action and all rest are one. So too prayer![78]

Several years ago I came across a passage in one of Andrew Murray's books, in which he suggests that we use our breathing as a way of quieting ourselves so that we can focus on our Lord Jesus Christ. Breath deeply, and as you exhale picture yourself releasing to God all your sin, your anxiety, and fears. And then as you inhale, see yourself breathing in the peace, forgiveness and power of God. It works. Try it. I did not know until recently that this practice comes from the Greek Orthodox tradition.

When I lived in England a few years ago I discovered the "Jesus Prayer", which also comes from the Orthodox tradition. It is a prayer that has many variations. The one I like is "Lord Jesus Christ, Son of the living God, have mercy on me, a sinner, redeemed through the precious blood of Jesus Christ, and grant me your peace." It can be shortened until it becomes simply the utterance of the sacred name: "Jesus." This is a prayer that is designed to be said over and over again until one finds that their heart is filled with the peace of God. Often in our seeking to pray we find ourselves so distracted that we are unable to really focus. The Jesus prayer, especially when said aloud, helps us to quiet ourselves and allow the sense of God's presence to become consciously ours. Many times I have used the Jesus prayer in conjunction with the breathing exercise, saying the name "Jesus" as I breath in and "peace" as I breath out. Thus summarizing the whole of the Jesus Prayer.

I have sometimes been disturbed by the emotional intensity of people who are seeking to experience the Holy Spirit. It seems so unrealistic and without staying power. They are often hot or cold and always seem to be seeking a new "spiritual high." When the Holy Spirit is relegated to "an experience," and as an experience generally something unusual, we never discover the depths of his peace and transforming power. While the Holy Spirit is certainly experienced, he is so much more than an experience. To experience the Spirit of God is not in itself a protection against spiritual struggle. Charles Spurgeon gave an exceptionally fine observation on the spiritual life, when he wrote:

> "It may be that there are saints who are always at their best and are happy enough never to lose the light of their Father's continence. I'm not sure there are such persons. For those believers with whom I have been most intimate have had a varied experience and those whom I have known who have boasted of their constant perfectness have not been the most reliable of individuals. I hope there is a spiritual region attainable where there are no clouds to hide the sun of our soul. But I cannot speak with positiveness, for I have never traversed that happy land. Every year of my life has had a winter as well as a summer and every day its night. I have hitherto seen clear shinings and heavy rains, and felt warm breezes and fierce winds. Speaking for the many of my brethren, I confess that though the substance be in us, as in the teal tree and the oak, yet we do lose our leaves, and the sap within us does not flow with equal vigor at all seasons. We have our downs as well as our ups, our valleys as well as our hills. We are not always rejoicing. We are sometimes in heaviness through manifold trials. Alas, we are grieved to confess that our fellowship with the Well-Beloved is not always that of a rapturous delight. But we have at times to seek him and cry, 'O, that I knew where I might find Him.' "[79]

If we can learn to keep ourselves in God's presence, we will discover that "relationship with God" which is both natural and fulfilling. The use of the breathing technique and the Jesus Prayer have helped me to relax and begin to really enjoy God. I haven't seen too many people who really seem to enjoy God! But when you do meet one, they are contagious! As the Westminster Confession puts it: "What is the chief end of mankind? The chief end of mankind is to glorify God and enjoy him forever." I am learning to enjoy God, and it is wonderful.

The mark of the servant of the Lord is the presence of the Holy Spirit. Rather than this being something that drives us into ourselves and separates us from the world in which we live, the Holy Spirit enhances our awareness of others and causes us to become involved in seeking to correct the hardness and injustice in our world. The next two qualities of a servant address this.

PRAYER PRINCIPLE # 15
As servants, we are marked by the presence of the Holy Spirit

What does living from the heart, or the center of our being mean to you? How do you personally make this a practice of your life?

What is the evidence in your life that the presence of the Holy Spirit is a reality? What effect does your presence have upon others?

What to you is the most amazing thing about the Holy Spirit?

3. The Servant of the Lord is Compassionate

One of the unfailing signs of a servant of the Lord is that s/he is sensitive to the hurts of others and have a passion to care and help. As Isaiah 42 puts it, *He will not shout or cry out, or raise his voice in the streets. A bruised reed he will not break, and a smoldering wick he will not snuff out.*

We live in a harsh world where noise and bluff and threats abound. There is not a one of us who has not been bruised and wounded by the actions of others that were intended to intimidate and keep us from becoming someone that might in some way threaten the other's position. Because of our self-centeredness and fears and sinfulness, the harshness which we have received we also dish out to others. You hurt me, so I hurt you back or if I can't hurt you, I will hurt someone else. Ah, sweet vengeance! How destructive it is! So the evil is passed on from one generation to another. Often the destructive action or attitude is unconscious and unintentional and seems to come from the hidden depths of our being and is our attempt to somehow deal with our own woundedness. It has often been observed that "hurting people, hurt people."

Paul instructed believers in Jesus Christ to break this cycle of evil. He instructs us, "Don't be overcome by evil, take the initiative, overcome evil with good (Romans 12:21 Phillips). This is possible because at the heart of the Gospel is the promise of healing for ourselves and then of our becoming a source of healing for others. In one of his great praise passages the Apostle Paul wrote: *Praise be to the God and Father of our Lord Jesus Christ, the Father of compassion and the God of all comfort; who comforts us in all our trouble so that we can comfort those in any trouble with the comfort we have received from God. For just as the sufferings of Christ flow over into our lives, so also through Christ our comfort overflows* (2 Corinthians 1:3-5). Christ's sufferings flow over into our lives giving us forgiveness, inner healing, cleansing, hope and peace. The comfort we have received flows out to others to bring encouragement, hope and strength. We bring Christ into the pain and distress of hurting people.

We receive the healing of God as we live from the center of our beings in reliance on the Spirit of Christ. As we allow the benefits of his sacrifice on our behalf to cleanse us, we receive his deep healing. As Isaiah said:

> *Surely he took up our infirmities and carried our sorrows, yet we considered him stricken by God, smitten by him, and afflicted. But he was pierced for our transgressions, he was crushed for our iniquities; the punishment that brought us peace was upon him, and by his wounds we are healed. (Isaiah 53:4-5).*

We seek his peace, which is wholeness, and his heart, which is compassionate love. To be in tune with the Master's heart means that we begin to see the world as he sees it. When Jesus preached his first sermon in his home town of Nazareth, Luke tells us that he read from the prophecy of Isaiah: *The Spirit of the Lord is on me, because he has anointed me to preach good news to the poor. He has sent me to proclaim freedom for the prisoners and recovery of sight for the blind, to release the oppressed, to proclaim the year of the Lord's favor.* (Luke 4:18-19. Luke seems to be quoting from some unknown Greek translation which varies from the Hebrew, which reads: *The Spirit of the Sovereign LORD is on me, because the LORD has anointed me to preach good news to the poor. He has sent me to bind up the brokenhearted, to proclaim freedom for the captives and release for the prisoners, to proclaim the year of the LORD's favor and the day of vengeance of our God, to comfort all who mourn* (Isaiah 61:1-2). The whole ministry of Jesus was the living out of the compassion of God as expressed in Isaiah 61. His ministry was one of seeking the lost, preaching, healing, and bringing hope. In his death and resurrection he accomplishes what we could not do for ourselves, he bears our sins and infirmities upon the cross so that we might be healed and set free. Having received from the Lord the benefits of salvation, we are set on the course of being his representatives in the world and embodying his compassion which we ourselves have so abundantly received.

James has an interesting statement about the need of mercy and compassion. He writes,

> *Speak and act as those who are going to be judged by the law that gives freedom, because judgment without mercy will be shown to anyone who has not been merciful. Mercy triumphs over judgment (James 2:12-13).*

Compassions has many aspects. It begins with awareness: awareness of ourselves and an awareness of others and an awareness of God. It is almost a truism that those who worship regularly are the most generous and most responsive to people who are in crisis. It is as though one's sensitivity to human need is heightened as one remembers the kindness and mercy of God which we ourselves have received.

"The word *compassion* is derived from the Latin words *pati* and *cum*, which together mean 'to suffer with.' Compassion asks us to go where it hurts, to enter into places of pain, to share in brokenness, fear, confusion, and anguish. Compassion challenges us to cry out with those in misery, to mourn with those who are lonely, to weep with those in tears. Compassion requires us to be weak with the weak, vulnerable with the vulnerable, and powerless with the powerless. Compassion means full immersion in the condition of being human. When we look at compassion this way, it becomes clear that something more is involved than a general kindness or tenderheartedness."[80]

This quotation may seem somewhat extreme, and has come out of the authors' reflection on the radical command of Jesus: *Be compassionate as you Father is compassionate* (Luke 6:36 JB). "This command does not restate the obvious, something we already wanted but had forgotten, an idea in line with our natural aspirations. On the contrary, it is a call that goes right against the grain; that turns us completely around and requires a total conversion of heart and mind. It is indeed a radical call, a call that goes to the roots of our lives" [81]

An example of awareness in Jesus is found in the account of John 9:1 ff., where we read, *As he passed by, he [Jesus] saw a man blind from his birth. And his disciples asked him, 'Rabbi, who sinned...that he was born blind?* The text makes a point that it was Jesus who saw the blind man and he must have pointed him out to the disciples who rather than seeing the man, see a theological problem: "Who sinned?"

It is Jesus, not the disciples, who has compassion. He brushes aside their question and simply states, *We must work the works of him who sent me, while it is day; night comes, when no one can work. (v. 4).* Compassion demands action not debate. Compassion is more than feeling sorry for someone, it is reaching out to them to do what we can to soften their misery.

But immediately we have a problem. There is so much suffering in the world and we do not have the resources, time, or energy to help everyone who may be suffering. In our world with its immediate view of human suffering through TV, the internet, etc., we can be overwhelmed by what has been called "compassion fatigue", which causes us to become insensitive to human need. Compassion is reduced to a feeling of pity, with the result that we do nothing. How do we deal with this?

Jesus makes a rather harsh statement to those who criticized the woman who anointed him with expensive perfume, *Why are you bothering this woman? She has done a beautiful thing to me. The poor you will always have with you...* (Matthew 26:10-11). There is never an end to need! I have always been fascinated by the story of Jesus walking through the area called the pool of Bethesda (John 5:1-10) where a great number of disabled people lay. In the midst of all this need, Jesus focused on only one man. Why did he not heal everyone there? The lesson I have learned from this is that I cannot help every person in need, nor is it God's purpose for me that I respond to every cry for help. If I am sensitive to the leading of the Holy Spirit who dwells within me, God can nudge me and let me know that this person is my responsibility. When I sense the nudging of the Spirit then I am expected to do what I can.

I have experienced God's nudgings many times in my ministry. One incident that remains very clear in my memory involved a elderly woman who was in the hospital because of an accident. She was not a member of my congregation and never attended church. I had visited her that morning. About the time I was getting ready to go home for supper, I felt such an urge to go back to the hospital that I acted on it. When I walked into her room, she said to me, "Pastor, how did you know I needed you?" That occasion was when she opened her heart to receive the forgiveness and peace of Christ and entered into a living relationship with Jesus as Lord. For the rest of her life, she recalled the significance of that visit, when I was able to lead her to the Savior.

Often , however, we have nothing to give and no way of alleviating the suffering. We feel helpless in the face of a situation which is beyond our ability to help. We have nothing to give and little to say -- sometimes even the promises in the Scripture seem almost a mockery. This is the very time when we must reach out, not with answers or "help", but by physically being present with the one who is suffering. The "ministry of presence" is often the most powerful ministry we do. As servants of the Lord, we bring the presence of the Holy Spirit--whether we are aware of it or not--and an assurance of God's care for this person. When we are out of our depth and have nothing of ourselves to give is the time when we become in an unusual way the very messenger of God. Jesus is called "Immanuel, God with us," and we become his physical presence, the embodiment of his loving compassion.

The Apostle Paul was often moved by compassion. In fact his passion to reach the lost was fired by his devotion to the Lord and his concern that everyone must know him. He writes: *I have great sorrow and unceasing anguish in my heart. For I could wish that I myself were cursed and cut off from Christ for the sake of my brothers, those of my own race, the people of Israel* Romans 9:2-4). *Brothers, my heart's desire and prayer to God for the Israelites is that they may be saved* Romans 10:1). *For, as I have often told you before and now say again even with tears, many live as enemies of the cross of Christ. Their end is destruction...*(Philippians 3:18-19). In 1Corinthians 9:19-23 Paul states his strategy for reaching the lost. He does it by identifying himself with their situation, whether they be Jew or Gentile, weak or strong, law keepers or without the law. He writes *I make myself a slave to everyone, to win as many as possible... I have become all things to all men so that by all possible means I might save some* (vv. 19, 22).

The servant of the Lord is characterized by compassionate love

PRAYER PRINCIPLE # 16

The Servant of the Lord is compassionate

Compassion was a characteristic of Jesus. In what way do you show compassion?

What is your experience of being nudged by God so that you know that he has put someone in your path through which he will show his love?

How do you deal with compassion fatigue?

4. The Servant of Lord is Concerned for Justice

In Isaiah 42:1-4 the emphasis on the servant establishing justice is the most prominent feature. I have underlined the parts relating to justice.

> *Here is my servant, whom I uphold, my chosen one in whom I delight; I will put my Spirit on him and he will bring justice to the nations. He will not shout or cry out, or raise his voice in the streets. A bruised reed he will not break, and a smoldering wick he will not snuff out. In faithfulness he will bring forth*

justice; he will not falter or be discouraged till he establishes justice on earth, In his law the islands will put their hope.

We need to understand that there is a difference between compassion and justice. Compassion is my personal response to another's suffering. Justice has to do with the establishment and preservation of equality of protection and opportunity before the law. Justice has to do with protecting people from those who are unscrupulous and would take advantage of and harm others for their own personal gain.

In their book *Compassion: A Reflection on the Christian Life,* the authors tell the following incident:

"One day, the three of us visited the late Hubert Humphrey to ask about compassion in politics. We had come because we felt he was one of the most caring human beings in the political arena. The Senator…was obviously caught off guard when asked how he felt about compassion in politics. Instinctively, he left his large mahogany desk…and joined us around a small coffee table. But then, after having adapted himself to the somewhat unusual situation, Senator Humphrey walked back to his desk, picked up a long pencil with a small eraser at its end, and said in his famous high-pitched voice: 'Gentlemen, look at this pencil. Just as the eraser is only a very small part of this pencil and is used only when you make a mistake, so compassion is only called upon when things get out of hand. The main part of life is competition; only the eraser is compassion. It is sad to say, gentlemen, put in politics compassion is just part of the competition.'"[82]

The authors go on to point out, "Perhaps this is how most of us really feel and think when we are honest with ourselves. Compassion is neither our central concern nor our primary stance in life." [83] They then go on to say that though this may be the way things are, it is not the way things are supposed to be from God's perspective. We are to *Be compassionate as your Father is compassionate* (Luke 6:36 JB).

Now I confess that I think Senator Humphrey was closer to the truth than the authors. It seems to me that one of the problems which we Christians have is our idealism which causes us to have an inability to separate private moral expectations from public moral decisions. Because we are called upon to be compassionate persons we assume that this also means that the state must be a compassionate state. If the primary concern of the state is to be compassionate, I do not see how there can be anything other than a striving for some kind of utopian society where no one owns anything and every one owns everything, and no one has less and no one has more than they need. As I understand the scriptures, not even heaven is completely free from distinctions between people. Both Jesus and Paul speak of God rewarding the faithful according to their deeds! And Jesus tells us that in heaven "the last will be first and the first last."

We need a society in which its citizens are compassionate and the government is concerned with justice in its establishment and execution of the laws and systems. Of course, when there are catastrophes the state can act with compassion for the victims. But when the state acts compassionately it is acting as an extension of the individual in that society.

The compassionate servant of the Lord must be concerned with justice because it is generally the weak, poor, and those on the edges of society who are most unable to claim and experience true justice. The "powerless" are always those who are least able to protect themselves and are easily over-looked or summarily dismissed from the conversations on what is societal justice and economic policy.

The problem is made more complex because every institution created by humans, whether it is the government of the state, the church, or the family, is inherently flawed so that the system itself perpetuates injustice or evil. Because of their self-interest, blindness and inability to accurately see the ramifications of decisions which are made, good compassionate individuals make and enforce laws and policies which are detrimental to segments of a population. An example that is commonly used is the American desire for low cost coffee and cheap bananas which helps to perpetuate poverty among the peasants in countries who grow coffee and bananas. Thus without even being aware of it, the common person in America helps to perpetuate subsistence living in another part of the world.

The civil rights struggle is a good example of systemic injustice and evil. Most white people did not want to prevent those with dark skins from achieving the freedom which education and economic success brings. They were, however, idealistically unaware that the very system with which they were comfortable worked against the rights of the black person. Racism is a systemic problem and is rooted in the way people think, believe and behave. The system (how things really work) perpetuates the injustice. It was only through the Herculean effort of people of compassion, like Dr. Martin Luther King, that the blindness, and selfishness of society was unmasked so that the injustice, hopelessness and unrighteousness of the plight of those who are of a minority race became obvious.

When Jesus attacked the Pharisees he was not condemning the actions of one person but the whole pharisaic system of moral behavior and thinking. When Paul condemns the church at Corinth for tolerating sinful behavior of one of their members, he was attacking, not some personal sin, but the whole church system that allowed the immoral behavior to continue unchallenged and uncondemned.

If the Christian community insists on regarding sin and evil as only a personal (and therefore private) issue, it will never be an agent for systemic change within a society. It is easy to condemn thievery while condoning those forces in society which contribute to the hopelessness and sense of helplessness that the less fortunate live with daily. There is always a need for the prophet who speaks out against the abuses, inadequacies, and injustices inherent in a system, and who seeks to rally support for change. Unfortunately, not every prophet is of God.

The servant of the Lord is concerned for justice for the poor, the oppressed, and the helpless. We are often overwhelmed by our own helplessness in the face of the system and feel that there is nothing we can do. Most of us are not prophets and do not feel called or able to lead a charge for changing some facet of the system that is unjust. We can, however, become involved with one person or family that has been beaten down by how things are. A saying which I memorized many years ago, has always motivated me: “I am only one, and I can’t do everything. But I am one, and I can do something. What I can do, I should do. What I should do, I will do.” There is an old story of a man walking along the beach, on which hundreds of star fish had been washed ashore. As the sun got hotter they would all die. He came upon a young man who was picking up star fish one at a time and throwing them back into the surf. The older man said, Son, there are so many star fish washed ashore, you can’t make any difference. The young man, stooping to pick up another star fish, answered, maybe not, but it makes a difference to that one, as he threw it back into the surf.

Because of our own weakness in the face of the system, we should fervently pray, as Jesus taught us: "Thy kingdom come, thy will be done on earth as it is in heaven." We should also pray that God would give us good judgment so that we can discern what we should be involved in, what we should support, and how we should do it. Let us never forget that our God is a God of justice and as his servants we a called to become engaged in the battle for right.

PRAYER PRINCIPLE # 17

The Christian should be concerned for justice.

Why should a follower of Christ be concerned for social justice?

What are some ways that we can be involved in the battle against injustice and inequality?

What must we guard against in being concerned for justice?

5. We serve the Lord by serving others

There is at least one more facet of being a servant of the Lord which is emphasized in the New Testament, especially by Jesus. We serve the Lord by serving others.

How do you love God, whom you cannot see, or serve the Lord who needs nothing from you? For a number of years I have been fascinated by the fact that in the New Testament there is a great deal said about God's love for us, but there is very little said about our love for God, and we are never commanded to love God, except in quotations from the Old Testament--Deuteronomy 6:4. John's statement in his first letter represents the perspective of the rest of the New Testament: *Dear friends, since God so loved us, we also ought to love one another* (1 John 4:11). We show our love to God by loving others, and we serve the Lord by giving our lives away in service to others in the name of Christ.

Jesus Christ himself provides the model. He instructed his disciples, *Whoever wants to become great among you must be your servant, and whoever wants to be first must be slave of all. For even the Son of Man did not come to be served, but to serve, and to give his life as a ransom for many* (Mark 10:43-45). And in the parable of the great judgment he says, *Whatever you did for the least of these brothers of mine, you did for me* (Matthew 25:40).

To serve others for Christ's sake is to live out in practical ways the compassion and mercy and kindness of our Lord. It is to be so abandoned to Jesus Christ that his call to meet the needs of others becomes more important than one's own comfort. It is to live out Paul's instructions in Philippians 2:1-7. *If you have any encouragement from being united with Christ, if any comfort from his love, if any fellowship with the Spirit, if any tenderness and compassion, then make my joy complete by being like-minded, having the same love, being one in spirit and purpose. Do nothing out of selfish ambition or vain conceit, but in humility consider others better than yourselves. Each of you should look not only to your own interests, but also to the interests of others. Your attitude should be the same as that of Christ Jesus: who, being in very nature God, did not consider equality with God something to be grasped, but made himself nothing, taking the very nature of a servant...*

To be a servant of Jesus Christ means that we are no longer our own, and have given up our right to ourselves, taking up our cross, and obediently follow him wherever he might lead (Mark 9:23). It is to be so controlled by the love of Christ that we begin to see the world around us through his eyes and have our hearts ache at the things that break his heart.

No one can be a true servant of the Lord in their own strength. To serve the Lord is more than doing, it has its power in being. It is a supernatural result of the transforming power of the Spirit that causes us to be conformed to more Christ-likeness. The servant is never aware of their Christ-likeness, they are only aware that they are obedient to Christ's call. Yet it is not simply what the servant does that brings glory to God, but rather what they are...the fact that Christ lives in them and they are living out their love for their Lord.

Appendix 1

Using Paul's prayers as a model or template for our own prayers

Sometimes it is difficult to know how to express what we are really wanting to pray. I believe there is great power in praying the Scripture. I find using the Scripture as a guide can greatly enhance my prayers both when I pray for myself and others. In this appendix I will limit myself to five of Paul's prayers and illustrate how I use them. Sometimes I keep very close to the Scripture, at other times I will branch out on some thought suggested to me and then return to the passage I am using as a template. Keeping myself tied to a passage of Scripture helps to maintain a momentum and direction to the prayer. I will begin with the Lord's Prayer which I regularly use in an expanded format which includes Paul's prayer in Ephesians 1:17-22.

The Lord's Prayer

Our Father who art in heaven, hallowed by your name (Father, I want to honor and magnify your name today, and may your name be praised throughout the world), **your kingdom come, your will be done on earth as it is in heaven** (May I do your will this day and please you more and more).

Give us this day our daily bread (thank you for your bountiful provision, your mercy, kindness, compassion and grace. I need your provision this day. I pray that you will especially bless ________ for they have been a channel of your blessings to me).

Forgive us our sins as we forgive those who sin against us. (Search me, O God, and know my heart, try me and know my thoughts, and see if there be any wicked way in me and lead me in the paths everlasting. Create in me a clean heart, O God, and renew in me a right spirit. Restore to me the joy of your salvation and grant me a willing and steadfast spirit to sustain me, and this day may the words of my mouth and the meditations of my heart be pleasing and acceptable to you, my strength and my redeemer.)

And lead us not into temptation (or a time of trial) **but deliver us from evil** (and the evil one. I need your protection, dear Father).

For yours is the kingdom and power and the glory forever. (May I praise you again and again this day. Open the eyes of my heart that I might be more aware of you goodness and glory. And I ask that you will give the Spirit of wisdom and revelation so that I might know you better. I also ask that you will enlighten me so that I will know the hope to which I have been called, your glorious inheritance in the saints, and your mighty power toward us who believe. That power is like the mighty strength you exerted when you raised Christ Jesus from the dead and made him to sit at your right hand in the heavenly realms, far above all the forces of evil and you made him to be head of over all things for the church, which is his body. And even when we were dead in our trespasses and sins you made us alive together with Christ. By grace we have been saved. And in him you made us to sit in the heavenly realms in Christ Jesus … Wow. Thank you, Dear Father. Let it be!). **Amen.**

2. Ephesians 1:3-11

There are times when I just want to praise God. Praise is one of the things I do not seem to do well. I am quick to give thanks but praise is a different category and I quickly run out of words. So I have found Ephesians 1 a very meaningful expression of the praise I feel, because it expresses so beautifully the mystery and greatness of God's purpose in Christ. With this passage I have just changed the pronouns to the 1st person singular and made other appropriate changes to make it flow.

I give praise to you, O God and Father of our Lord Jesus Christ, for you have blessed me in the heavenly realms with every spiritual blessing in Christ. For you chose me in him before the creation of the world to be holy and blameless in your sight. In love you predestined me to be adopted as your child through Jesus Christ, in accordance with your pleasure and will--to the praise of your glorious grace, which you have freely given me in the One you love. In Christ I have redemption through his blood, the forgiveness of sins, in accordance with the riches of God's grace that you lavished on me with all wisdom and understanding. And you made known to your people the mystery of your will according to you good pleasure, which you purposed in Christ--to bring all things in heaven and on together under one head, even Christ. Jesus is Lord!

In him I was also chosen, having been predestined according to your plan, O God, for you work out everything in conformity with the purpose of your will, in order that I might live to the praise of your glory. And you marked me in Christ with a seal, the promised Holy Spirit, who is a deposit guaranteeing my inheritance until the redemption of those who are God's possession--to the praise of your glory.

3. Ephesians 3:14-21

I have often used the prayer in Ephesians 3 when praying for my children and individuals in my congregation. Using this model has enabled me to pray about the truly important things.

I bow in reverence before you, dear Father, whose heart embraces every person. I pray for __________, and ask that out of your glorious riches you may strengthen them with power through you Holy Spirit in their inner beings. I pray that they might receive your love and grace so that Christ will dwell in their hearts through faith. I ask, dear Father, that they will be rooted and established in love and that they will make good friends with whom they can grow in understanding and commitment to your will so that together they can grasp something of the mystery and greatness of who you are -- how wide and long and high and deep, and so know by experience the love of Christ that surpasses knowledge--that they may truly be a man or woman of God, filled with the measure of the fullness of God. Being blessed by you and blessing others in Jesus' Name.

Now to you, Heavenly Father, who is able to do immeasurably more than all I ask or imagine, according to you power at work within us, to you be glory in the church and in Christ Jesus for ever and ever. Amen.

4. Philippians 1:9-11

The prayer in Philippians 1 is one I have often prayed for couples who are getting married and for marriages that are struggling.

Gracious and holy heavenly Father, I pray that the love of ________ and ___________ for one another may grow more and more in knowledge and depth of insight, so that they may be able to discern what is best and may be pure and blameless until the day of Christ. I ask you to fill them with the fruit of righteousness that comes through Jesus Christ--to the glory and praise of God.

5. Colossians 1:9-12

There are times when I am concerned with what I can only call "the sloppy life-style" of people who seem to be conforming to the ways of the world to the detriment of their own spiritual relationship with Christ. The vitality of the spiritual life is often determined by the orientation of the will. It is so easy to be critical and judgmental and I have found Paul's prayer in Colossians 1 a help to express in positive terms my concern.

Dear Heavenly Father, I pray that you will give to _______________ heightened spiritual wisdom and deepened understanding so that they will be filled with the knowledge of your will and intentions so that they will be motivated to live a life that is worthy of the Lord Jesus Christ, who died for them. I pray that they will desire to seek to please their Lord in all they do. Father, help them to make good choices so they will bear good fruit and grow in the knowledge of God. And I ask you to strengthen them with your power so that they will have great endurance and patience, and live joyfully, giving thanks to you, Father, for you have qualified them to share in the inheritance of the saints in the kingdom of light. I pray that they will not take for granted the redemption and forgiveness which is theirs in Jesus Christ. I also ask you to strengthen their hearts so that they will be blameless and holy in the presence of our God and Father when our Lord Jesus comes. (This last request is from 1 Thessalonians 3:13).

Appendix 2

ALL THE REFERENCES TO PRAYER IN PAUL'S LETTERS

In the order in which they appear in our Bibles
The text of these references is printed in Appendix 3

Romans 1:7	Salutation
Romans 1:8-10	Thanks/general
Romans 1:21-23	Failure to be thankful
Romans 1:25	Doxology
Romans 5:11	Praise
Romans 7:24-25	Praise
Romans 8:15-17	Instruction
Romans 8:26-27	Instruction
Romans 8:34	Instruction
Romans 9:5	Doxology
Romans 10:1-3	Intercession
Romans 10:13-15	General
Romans 11:33-36	Doxology
Romans 14:6	Thanks
Romans 15:5-6	Wish prayer/Benedictory Blessing
Romans 15:7-12	Praise
Romans 15:13	Wish prayer/Benedictory Blessing
Romans 15:17-19	Praise
Romans 15:30-33	Request for prayer/blessing
Romans 16:25-27	Benedictory blessing/doxology
1 Corinthians 1:3	Salutation
1 Corinthians 1:4-7	Thanks
1 Corinthians 7:5	General
1 Corinthians 10:29b-30	Thanks

1 Corinthians 11:4-5, 13	Instruction
1 Corinthians 11:23b-24	Thanks
1 Corinthians 14:8-,28	Instructions
1 Corinthians 15:57	Praise
1 Corinthians 16:22	General
1 Corinthians 16:23-24	Benedictory Blessing
2 Corinthians 1:2	Salutation
2 Corinthians 1:3-5	Praise
2 Corinthians 1:20	Instruction
2 Corinthians 2:14	Praise
2 Corinthians 4:15	Thanks
2 Corinthians 8:16-17	Thanks
2 Corinthians 9:11-15	General/Praise
2 Corinthians 10:4-5	Instruction
2 Corinthians 11:30-31	Praise
2 Corinthians 12:7-9	General
2 Corinthians 13:7	General
2 Corinthians 13:13	Wish prayer/BenedictoryBlessing
Galatians 1:3-5	Salutation/Doxology
Galatians 1:23-24	Praise
Galatians 4:4-7	Instruction
Galatians 4:19-20	Intercession
Galatians 6:6-18	Benedictory Blessing
Ephesians 1:2	Salutation
Ephesians 1:3-14	Praise
Ephesians 1:15-20	Prayer Report
Ephesians 2:18	Instruction
Ephesians 3:12	Instruction
Ephesians 3:14-21	Prayer Report
Ephesians 5:19-20	Instruction
Ephesians 6:18, 19-20	Instruction/Request
Ephesians 6:23-24	Benedictory blessing
Philippians 1:2	Salutation
Philippians 1:3-6	Thanks
Philippians 1:9-11	Prayer Report
Philippians l:18b-20	Praise

Philippians 4:4, 6-7	Instruction
Philippians 4:19-20	Doxology
Philippians 4:23	Benedictory blessing
Colossians 1:2	Salutation
Colossians 1:3-6a	Thanks
Colossians 1:9-14	Prayer Report
Colossians 2:1-4	Intercession
Colossians 3:15-17	Thanks
Colossians 4:2-4	Instruction
Colossians 4:12	Intercession
Colossians 4:18	Request/Benedictory Blessing
1 Thessalonians 1:1	Salutation
1 Thessalonians 1:2-3	Thanks
1 Thessalonians 2:13-14	Thanks
1 Thessalonians 3:11-13	Wish prayer
1 Thessalonians 5:16-18	Instruction
1 Thessalonians 5:23-24	Wish prayer/Benedictory Blessing
1 Thessalonians 5:25	Request/Benedictory Blessing
2 Thessalonians 1:2	Salutation
2 Thessalonians 1:3-4	Thanks
2 Thessalonians 1:11-12	Prayer report
2 Thessalonians 2:13-14	Thanks
2 Thessalonians 2:16-17	Wish prayer
2 Thessalonians 3:1-2	Prayer request
2 Thessalonians 3:5	Wish prayer
2 Thessalonians 3:16, 18	Wish/benediction
1 Timothy 1:2	Salutation
1 Timothy 1:12-13	Thanks
1 Timothy 1:15-17	Doxology
1 Timothy 2:1-4	Instruction
I Timothy 2:8	Instruction
1 Timothy 6:14-16	Doxology
1 Timothy 6:21	Benedictory Blessing
2 Timothy 1:2	Salutations
2 Timothy 1:3-5	Thanks

2 Timothy 1:15-18	Intercession
2 Timothy 2:22	General
2 Timothy 4:16-18	Praise/doxology
2 Timothy 4:22	Benedictory Blessing
Titus 1:4	Salutation
Titus 3:15	Benedictory Blessing
Philemon 3	Salutation
Philemon 6-7	Intercession
Philemon 22	General
Philemon 25	Benedictory Blessing

APPENDIX 3

THE PRAYER REFERENCES

ARRANGED ACCORDING TO SUBJECT
Sections D through J are annotated

Appendix 3 A: Prayer Reports

When we think of the prayers of the Apostle Paul we generally mean, what the scholars call, his prayer reports. These prayer reports are rich in content. In these prayer reports the Apostle records, not the actual words, but rather the themes which comprise his prayers for his friends to which the various letters were sent. Because I comment on them in the text of the book I will only list them here without comment.

Ephesians 1:15-20 - Prayer Report
For this reason, ever since I heard about your faith in the Lord Jesus and your love for all the saints, I have not stopped giving thanks for you, remembering you in my prayers. I keep asking that the God of our Lord Jesus Christ, the glorious Father, may give you the Spirit of wisdom and revelation, so that you may know him better. I pray also that the eyes of your heart may be enlightened in order that you may know the hope to which he has called you, the riches of his glorious inheritance in the saints, and his incomparably great power for us who believe. That power is like the working of his mighty strength, which he exerted in Christ when he raised him from the dead and seated him at his right hand in the heavenly realms...

Ephesians 3:14-21 - Prayer Report

For this reason I kneel before the Father, from whom his whole family in heaven and on earth derives its name. I pray that out of his glorious riches he may strengthen you with power through his Spirit in your inner being, so that Christ may dwell in your hearts through faith. And I pray that you, being rooted and established in love, may have power, together with all the saints, to grasp how wide and long and high and deep is the love of Christ, and to know this love that surpasses knowledge—that you may filled to the measure of all the fullness of God. Now to him who is able to do immeasurably more than all we ask or imagine, according to his power that is at work within us, to him be glory in the church and in Christ Jesus throughout all generations, for ever and ever! Amen.

Philippians 1:9-11 - Prayer Report

And this is my prayer: that your love may abound more and more in knowledge and depth of insight, so that you may be able to discern what is best and may be pure and blameless until the day of Christ, filled with the fruit of righteousness that comes through Jesus Christ--to the glory and praise of God

Colossians 1:9-14 - Prayer Report

For this reason, since the day we heard about you, we have not stopped praying for you and asking God to fill you with the knowledge of his will through all spiritual wisdom and understanding. And we pray this in order that you may live a life worthy of the Lord and may please him in every way: bearing fruit in every good work, growing in the knowledge of God, being strengthened with all power according to his glorious might so that you may have great endurance and patience, and joyfully giving thanks to the Father, who has qualified you to share in the inheritance of the saints in the kingdom of light. For he has rescued us from the dominion of darkness and brought us into the kingdom of the Son he loves, in whom we have redemption, the forgiveness of sins.

2 Thessalonians 1:11-12 - Prayer report
With this in mind, we constantly pray for you, that our God may count you worthy of his calling, and that by his power he may fulfill every good purpose of yours and every act prompted by your faith. We pray this so that the name of our Lord Jesus may be glorified in you, and you in him, according to the grace of our God and the Lord Jesus Christ.

APPENDIX 3 B: SALUTATIONS

Rom 1:7	*Grace and peace to you from God our Father and from the Lord Jesus Christ.*
1 Cor 1:3	*Grace and peace to you from God our Father and theLord Jesus Christ.*
2 Cor 1:2	*Grace and peace to you from God our Father and the Lord Jesus Christ.*
Gal 1:3-5	*Grace and peace to you from God our Father and the Lord Jesus Christ, who gave himself for our sins to rescue us from the present evil age, according to the will of our God and Father, to whom be glory for ever and ever. Amen.*
Eph 1:2	*Grace and peace to you from God our Father and the Lord Jesus Christ.*
Phil 1:2	*Grace and peace to you from God our Father and the Lord Jesus Christ.*
Col 1:2	*Grace and peace to you from God our Father.*
1 Thes 1:1	*To the church of the Thessalonians in God the Father and the Lord Jesus Christ: Grace and peace to you.*
2 Thes 1:2	*Grace and peace to you from God the Father and the Lord Jesus Christ.*
1 Tim 1:2	*Grace, mercy and peace from God the Father and Christ Jesus our Lord.*
2 Tim 1:2	*Grace, mercy and peace from God the Father and Christ Jesus our Lord.*

Titus 1:4	*Grace and peace from God the Father and Christ Jesus our Savior.*
Phil 3	*Grace to you and peace from God our Father and the Lord Jesus Christ.*

APPENDIX 3 C: BENEDICTORY BLESSINGS

Romans 15:5-6 - *May the God who gives endurance and encouragement give you a spirit of unity among yourselves as you follow Christ Jesus, so that with one heart and mouth you may glorify the God and Father of our Lord Jesus Christ.*

Romans 15:13 - *May the God of hope fill you with all joy and peace as you trust in him, so that you may overflow with hope by the power of the Holy Spirit.*

Romans 15:30-33 - *I urge you, brothers, by our Lord Jesus Christ and by the love of the Spirit, to join me in my struggle by praying to God for me. Pray that I may be rescued from the unbelievers in Judea and that my service in Jerusalem may be acceptable to the saints there, so that by God's will I may come to you with joy and together with you be refreshed. The God of peace be with you all. Amen.*

Romans 16:25-27 - *Now to him who is able to establish you by my gospel and the proclamation of Jesus Christ, according to the revelation of the mystery hidden for long ages past, but now revealed and made known through the prophetic writings by the command of the eternal God, so that all nations might believe and obey him--to the only wise God be glory forever through Jesus Christ! Amen.*

1 Corinthians 16:23-24 - *The grace of the Lord Jesus be with you. My love to all of you in Christ Jesus. Amen.*

2 Corinthians 13:14 - *May the grace of the Lord Jesus Christ, and the love of God, and the fellowship of the Holy Spirit be with you all.*

Galatians 6:16, 18 - *Peace and mercy to all who follow this rule, even to the Israel of God. . . The grace of our Lord Jesus Christ be with your spirit, brothers. Amen*

Ephesians 6:23-24 - *Peace to the brothers, and love with faith from God the Father and the Lord Jesus Christ. Grace to all who love our Lord Jesus Christ with an undying love.*

Philippians 4:23 - *The grace of the Lord Jesus Christ be with your spirit. Amen.*

Colossians 4:18 - *I, Paul, write this greeting in my own hand. Remember my chains. Grace be with you.*

1 Thessalonians 5:23-24 - *May God himself, the God of peace, sanctify you through and through. May your whole spirit, soul and body be kept blameless at the coming of our Lord Jesus Christ. The one who calls you is faithful and he will do it.*

1 Thessalonians 5:25 - *Brothers, pray for us. Grace and peace to you from God the Father and the Lord Jesus Christ.*

2 Thessalonians 3:16, 18 - *Now may the Lord of peace himself give you peace at all times and in every way. The Lord be with all of you. . . The grace of our Lord Jesus Christ be with you all.*

1 Timothy 6:21 - *Grace be with you.*

2 Timothy 4:22 - *The Lord be with your spirit. Grace be with you.*

Titus 3:15 *Grace be with you all.*

Philemon 25 - *The grace of the Lord Jesus Christ be with your spirit.*

Appendix 3D

Instructions

With annotations

Romans 8:15-17

For you did not receive a spirit that makes you a slave again in fear, but you received the Spirit of sonship. And by him we cry "Abba, Father. The Spirit himself testifies with our spirit that we are God's children. Now if we are children, then we are heirs—heirs of God and co-heirs with Christ, if indeed we share in his sufferings in order that we may also share in his glory.

The deep, profound, intense realization that God is not just Father, but Abba, Father, my Father -- Abba is a term that is a picture of a child's intimate certainty of a father's love. This deep consciousness is the Holy Spirit's testimony to us that we are truly children of God, members of his family through Jesus Christ, and thus heirs together with our Lord.

Romans 8:26-27

In the same way, the Spirit helps us in our weakness. We do not know what we ought to pray, but the Spirit himself intercedes for us with groans that words

These verses are a wonderful encouragement to us who pray. It affirms that prayer is not just our activity but that God is active to make our prayer effective. Because we are weak and without full understanding, *cannot express, And he who searches our hearts knows the mind of the Spirit, because the Spirit intercedes for the saints in accordance with God's will.*

The Spirit helps us. We do not know for what we ought to pray or ask. The Spirit knows our heart's desire and intercedes in accordance with God's will.

Romans 8:34

Who is he that condemns? Christ Jesus, who died— more than that, who was raised to life—is at the right hand of God and is also interceding for us.

It is important for us to know that our Lord continues to intercede for us.

1 Corinthians 11:4-5, 13

Now I want you to realize that the head of every man is Christ, and the head of the woman is man, and the head of Christ is God. Every man who prays or prophesies with his had covered dishonors his head. And every woman who prays or prophesies with her head uncovered dishonors her head—it is just as though her head were shaved... Judge for your selves: Is it proper for a woman to pray to God with her head uncovered?

This is a difficult passage and it may be hard for us to see how it relates to us today.

Verse 13 would seem to indicate that the instruction regarding the necessity of a woman having her head covered when praying was cultural in nature rather than revelational. However, the principle of the need for humility in prayer and sensitivity to the cultural mores is one that is important and applicable to us today.

1 Corinthians 14:14-18, 28

For this reason the man who speaks in a tongue should pray that he may interpret what he says. For if I pray in a tongue, my spirit prays, but my mind is unfruitful. So what shall I do? I will pray with my spirit, but I will also pray with my mind; otherwise...how can one who finds himself among those who do not understand say "Amen" to your thanksgiving, since he does not know what you are saying. You may be giving thanks well enough, but the man is not edified. I thank God that I speak in tongues more than all of you. But in the church I would rather speak five intelligible words to instruct others than ten thousand words in a tongue.

If there is no interpreter the speaker should keep quiet in the church and speak to himself and God.

Instructions regarding speaking tongues in a communal -- church -- setting.

Unless there is one present who has the gift of interpretation, one should keep silent and speak to himself and God. For while speaking in tongues edifies the speaker, it has no value to others unless they can understand what is said.

2 Corinthians 1:20

For no matter how many promises God has made, they are "Yes" in Christ. And so through him the "Amen" is spoken by us to the glory of God.

As we claim the promises of God, God is glorified, for in Christ they do belong to us as well as to the original recipients of the promises. Christ is God's "Yes"!

2 Corinthians 10:4-5

The weapons we fight with are not the weapons of the world. On the contrary, they have divine power to demolish strongholds. We demolish arguments and every pretension that sets itself up against the knowledge of God, and we take captive every thought to make it obedient to Christ.

Prayer is not a safe, easy endeavor. It is one of the tools or weapons which God has provided that enables us to engage the enemy with strength and authority.

Galatians 4:4-7

But when the time had fully come, God sent his Son, born of a woman, born under law, to redeem those under law, that we might receive the full rights of sons. Because you are sons, God sent the Spirit of his Son into our hearts, the Spirit who calls out, "Abba, Father." So you are no longer a slave, but a son...

The assurance of the Spirit that causes us to call out to God as *Abba*, Father, is his confirming evidence that we are really God's children.

Ephesians 2:18
For through him (Christ) we both have access to the Father by one Spirit.

Ephesians 3:12
In him and through faith in him we may approach God with freedom and confidence.

Ephesians 5:19-20
Speak to one another with psalms, hymns and spiritual songs. Sing and make music in your heart to Lord, always giving thanks to God the Father for everything, in the name of our Lord Jesus Christ.

Ephesians 6:18, 19-20
And pray in the Spirit on all occasions with all kinds of prayers and requests. With this in mind, be alert and always keep on praying for all the saints. Pray also for me that whenever I

Christian prayer is Trinitarian in nature. We come to God through Jesus Christ and are given access to the Father by the Spirit. Thus in prayer we are given the privilege of participating in the perfect worship which Jesus and the Spirit give to the Father.

Although we are his redeemed children, we come to the Father in the name of our Lord Jesus Christ. In prayer we are given the privilege of participating in Christ's perfect worship, adoration and praise to the Father

That is why we sing and make music in our hearts to God as we express our thanks for all he has done and given us.

open my mouth, words may be given me so that I will fearlessly make known the mystery of the gospel, for which I am an ambassador in chains. Pray that I may declare it fearlessly, as I should.

.

"We are to pray in the power of the Spirit. Praying in the Spirit does not refer specifically to praying in tongues, though it may include glossalalia. Christian prayer is dependent on and energized by God's Spirit. We are to be alert for we do not drift into prevailing prayer by accident" (Leon Morris). We need to be alert because we are in a battle against Satan's schemes and all the forces of evil (Eph. 6:10-11). We are not in this battle alone but need to pray constantly for all the saints. "No soldier entering battle prays for himself alone, but for all his fellow-soldiers also. They form one army, and the success of one is the success of all" (Charles Hodge).

Philippians 4:4, 6-7

Rejoice in the Lord always. I will say it again: Rejoice!... Do not be anxious about anything, but in everything, by prayer and petition, with thanksgiving, present your requests to God And the peace of God, which transcends all understanding, will guard your hearts and your minds in Christ Jesus.

Prayer with thanksgiving to God is the antidote to worry and anxiety. Paul strings together several words that are really synonyms to describe prayer. Each of these words carry the thrust of requesting something from God and not just praising him. The promise is that we will experience God's peace and our hearts will be guarded and kept in Christ Jesus.

Colossians 3:15-17

Let the peace of Christ rule in your hearts, since as members of one body you were called to peace. And be thankful. Let the word of Christ dwell in you richly as you teach and admonish one another with all wisdom, and as you sing psalms, hymns and spiritual songs with gratitude in your hearts to God. And whatever you do, whether in word or deed, do it all in the name of the Lord Jesus, giving thanks to God the Father through him.

Several principles of prayer are found here:

1. Effective prayer is offered out of a life that puts Christ at the center.
2. Seeks to be at peace with others.
3. Nourishes itself in God's word so that the pray-ers can encourage and instruct one another.
4. This prayer has a deep gratitude to God.
5. The whole life is a prayer offered to God in praise and thanksgiving.
6. The object of prayer is God the Father and given in the name of the Lord Jesus.

Colossians 4:2-4

Devote yourselves to prayer, being watchful and thankful. And pray for us, too, that God may open a door for our message, so that we may proclaim the mystery of Christ, for which 1 am in chains. Pray that I may proclaim it clearly, as I should.

The vital Christian life is one of continuous commitment to prayer. The life of prayer is marked by an alertness to the signs of the times, Satan's schemes and is to be done in a spirit of thankfulness. Praying for others is a natural and necessary part of prayer.

1 Thessalonians 5:16-18

Be joyful always; pray continually; give thanks in all circumstances, for this is God's will for you in Christ Jesus.

A joyful spirit, prayer and the expressions of gratitude, no matter what the circumstances is characteristic of Christian prayer. See Acts 16 with its description of Paul and Silas in prison in Philippi.

1 Timothy 2:1-4

I urge, then, first of all, that requests, prayers, intercession and thanksgiving be made for everyone—for kings and all those in authority, that we may live peaceful and quiet lives in all godliness and holiness. This is good, and pleases God our Savior, who wants all men to be saved and to come to a knowledge of the truth.

Praying for others, including the movers and shakers of society is a responsibility which Christians should take seriously. It affects the peace in which we live and honors God, whose desire is that everyone recognize and follow Jesus Christ as Savior and Lord.

I Timothy 2:8

I want men everywhere to lift up holy hands in prayer, without anger or disputing.

Posture in prayer can be important. Paul mentions two postures --kneeling, Eph. 3:14 and here, the raising of the hands. The raising of the hands to God can be an act of praise, an attitude that we are ready to receive, or an act of imploring God to do something. At any rate, the lifting of the hands add an intensity to one's praying

However, if there is anger in our hearts or dissension with a fellow Christian, it becomes an act of hypocrisy (see Matthew 5:24).

Appendix 3 E:
Doxology and Praise

Peppered throughout his letters are phrases which I have designated as Doxology. A doxology is a special form of praise to God. All but one are addressed to God and not Jesus.

Praises are more general in nature.

Romans 1:25
They exchanged the truth of God for a lie, and worshiped and served created things rather than the Creator—who is forever praised. Amen.

The thought of those who reject the living God who created all things causes Paul to break out in praise to the Creator whom the world has rejected.

Romans 7:24-25
What a wretched man I am! Who will rescue me from this body of death? Thanks be to God—through Jesus Christ our Lord!

The very thought of his own weakness and wretchedness apart from Christ, causes Paul to express his gratitude to God, who has given Jesus Christ our Lord to rescue us from our plight.

Romans 9:5

Theirs are the patriarchs, and from them is traced the human ancestry of Christ, who is God over all, forever praised! Amen.

There is some controversy over how one should translate the last phrase. NIV footnotes suggest two other possibilities: (1) *Christ, who is over all, God be forever praised!* (2) *Christ, God who is over all be forever praised.*

If the NIV is accepted, this is the only place where Christ is called God in Paul's writing, which makes this translation suspect. In light of Paul's many other statements, probably #2 is to be preferred.

No matter how one translates this verse, God's faithfulness to Israel and the privilege he gave them of bringing the Messiah--Christ -- calls forth praise.

Romans 1 1:33-36

Oh, the depth of the riches of the wisdom and knowledge of God! How unsearchable his judgments, and his paths beyond tracing out! "Who has known the mind of the Lord? Or who has been his counselor? " "Who has ever given to God that God should repay him?" For from him and through him and to him are all things. To him be the glory forever! Amen.

This pageant of praise is a patina of allusions to and quotations from the OT –Isaiah, Job and Jeremiah. The last verse is an echo of what Paul wrote in 1 Corinthians 8:6.

As Paul thinks about the mystery of God's ways it causes him to bow in wonder before him and express his praise

Romans 15:7-12

Accept one another, then, just as Christ accepted you, in order to bring praise to God. For I tell you that Christ has become a servant to the Jews on behalf of God's truth, to confirm the promises made to the patriarchs so that the Gentiles may glorify God for his mercy, as it is written: "Therefore I will praise you among the Gentiles; I will sing hymns to your name." Again it says, "Rejoice, O Gentiles, with his people." And again,

This is not a praise by Paul but rather an encouragement to these Romans to do that which will cause praise to be given to God.

Because Christ has accepted them, Jewish and Gentile Christians should accept one another. By so doing, they confirm God's promises in the OT that salvation is for the Gentiles as well as the Jews. This will cause Gentiles to praise and honor God.

"Praise the Lord, all you Gentiles, and sing praises to him, all you peoples." And again, Isaiah says, "The root of Jesse will spring up, one who will arise to rule over the nations; the Gentiles will hope in him."

Romans 15:17-19
Therefore I glory in Christ Jesus in my service to God. I will not venture to speak of any thing except what Christ has accomplished through me in leading the Gentiles to obey God by what I have said and done—by the power of signs and miracles, through the power of the Spirit. So from Jerusalem all the way around to Illyricum, I have fully proclaimed the gospel of Christ.

In these verses we have Paul rejoicing in Christ because of God's blessing upon his ministry. This is not so much a boast as it is an expression of extreme wonder that he has been an instrument that God has used. When one realizes that God has been able to accomplish something through him/her, the result is never pride, but rather sheer wonder.

1 Corinthians 15:57
But thanks be to God! He gives us the victory through our Lord Jesus Christ. Therefore, my dear brothers, stand firm...

As Paul thinks of what the resurrection of Christ means, he breaks into praise to God who has given us the victory through our Lord Jesus Christ. As is usual for Paul, he sees practical

2 Corinthians 1:3-5

Praise be to the God and Father of our Lord Jesus Christ, the Father of compassion and the God of all comfort, who comforts us in all our troubles, so that we can comfort those in any trouble with the comfort we ourselves have received from God. For just as the sufferings of Christ flow over into our lives, so also through Christ our comfort overflows.

implications that come from this truth – *Therefore stand firm.*

As Paul prepares to mention his own special time of distress he gives praise *to the God and Father of our Lord Jesus Christ, the Father of compassion and the God of all comfort.* He is speaking out of his own experience which confirmed what he knew—that Christ is present in the midst of our sufferings and enables the comfort and encouragement and hope which we receive to overflow so that we become a source of blessing and faith to others experiencing trouble.

2 Corinthians 2:14

But thanks be to God, who always leads us in triumphal procession in Christ and through us spreads everywhere the fragrance of the knowledge of him.

Paul cannot help but give thanks when he thinks of how God has transformed his life and made him an example of the triumphant love of our Lord Jesus Christ.

2 Corinthians 9:11-15

You will be made rich in every way so that you can be generous on every occasion, and through us your generosity will result in thanksgiving to God. This service that you perform is not only supplying the needs of God's people but is also overflowing in many expressions of thanks to God. Because of the service by which you have proved yourselves, men will praise God for the obedience that accompanies your confession of the gospel of Christ, and for your generosity in sharing with them and with everyone else. And in their prayers for you their hearts will go out to you, because of the surpassing grace God has given you. Thanks be to God for his indescribable gift.

Paul's exclamation: *Thanks be to God for his indescribable gift,* is for him the natural result of his realizing anew that when people respond to Christ's love by generously sharing God's blessings with others, gratitude and praise to God are multiplied. There develops a mutual concern of prayer for one another because of the abundant grace of God.

2 Corinthians 11:30-31

If I must boast, I will boast of the things that show my weakness. The God and Father of the Lord Jesus, who is to be praised for ever, knows that I am not lying.

At a time when Paul feels it necessary to call upon God as his witness to truth, he finds himself breaking out into a short exclamation of praise. This praise is probably a reflection of Paul's Jewish and rabbinical heritage, where the very mention of God was often

Galatians 1:3-5

Grace and peace to you from God our Father and the Lord Jesus Christ, who gave himself for our sins to rescue us from the present evil age, according to the will of our God and Father, to whom be glory for ever and ever. Amen.

Galatians 1:23-24

They only heard the report: "The man who formerly persecuted us is now preaching the faith he once tried to destroy." And they praised God because of me.

Ephesians 1:3-14

Praise be to the God and Father of our Lord Jesus Christ, who has blessed us in the heavenly realms with every spiritual blessing in Christ. For he chose us in him before the creation of the world to be holy and blameless in his

followed by an expression of praise.

This doxology is probably a reflection of Paul's Jewish heritage. But it is more than a formality--Paul never ceased to be amazed at the redemptive grace and love of God so vividly expressed in Christ's suffering and death.

God's people cannot help but give praise when they hear of a life transformed by faith in Jesus Christ.

It has often been observed that this whole passage is almost in the form of a prayer. By changing the references to God from the 3rd to the 2nd person and making the appropriate changes this would require, it reads like a prayer of praise.

sight. In love he predestined us to be adopted as his sons through Jesus Christ, in accordance with his pleasure and will-- to the praise of his glorious grace, which he has freely given us in the One he loves. In him we have redemption through his blood, the forgiveness of sins, in accordance with the riches of God's grace that he lavished on us with all wisdom and understanding. And he made known to us the mystery of his will according to his good pleasure, which he purposed in Christ, to be put into effect when the times will have reached their fulfillment—to bring all things in heaven and earth together under one head, even Christ.

In him we were also chosen, having been predestined according to the plan of him who works out everything in conformity with the purpose of his will, in order that we. who were the first to hope in Christ, might be for the praise of this glory. And you also were included in

Prayer is such a vital part of the whole book of Ephesians that it might be referred to as theology on its knees.

Ephesians 1:3-14 is a great pageantry of praise to God.

Paul strains at language to express his wonder at what God has done in Christ because of his great love for us.

Among other things he praises God for the following things:

-- He chose us in Christ to be holy and blameless in his sight.

-- He predestined us to be adopted as his children through Jesus Christ.

-- He has expressed his pleasure and will in his glorious grace freely given us in the One he loves.

-- We are redeemed and our sins forgiven out of the riches of his grace that he lavished upon us.

Christ when you heard the word of truth, the gospel of your salvation. Having believed, you were marked in him with a seal, the promised Holy Spirit, who is a deposit guaranteeing our inheritance until the redemption of those who are God's possession—to the praise of his glory.

Philippians l:18b-20
Yes, and I will continue to rejoice, for I know that through your prayers and the help given by the Spirit of Jesus Christ, what has happened to me will turn out for my deliverance. I eagerly expect and hope that I will in no way be ashamed, but will have sufficient courage so that now as always Christ will be exalted in my body, whether by life or by death.

Philippians 4:19-20
And my God will meet all your needs according to his glorious riches in Christ Jesus. To our

-- He has disclosed to us the mystery of his will, i.e., to bring all things under the Lordship of Christ.
-- He has done all this that we might be to the praise of his glory.
-- He has put the seal of his ownership upon us--the promised Holy Spirit.
-- The Holy Spirit is God's guarantee of our inheritance with the redeemed.

It is interesting to observe the Apostle making a deliberate choice to rejoice in the face of adverse circumstances. He knows he can count on his friends and God to bring him through to deliverance. His desire is to glorify God no matter what happens to him.

When Paul thinks of God's abundant provision and faithfulness it calls forth from him a doxology of worship, honor and praise.

God and Father be glory for ever and ever. Amen.	
1 Timothy 1:15-17 *Here is a trustworthy saying that deserves full acceptance: Christ Jesus came into the world to save sinners—of whom I am the worst. But for that very reason 1 was shown mercy so that in me, the worst of sinners, Christ Jesus might display his unlimited patience as an example for those who would believe on him and receive eternal life. Now to the King eternal, immortal, invisible, the only God, be honor and glory for ever and ever. Amen.*	Paul rejoices that he is living, personal proof that Christ Jesus came into the world to save sinners! His transformed life shows that no matter what we have done, God is patient and merciful and will give eternal life to all who believe. This causes him to give a formal doxological statement in praise to God.
1 Timothy 6:14-16 *Keep this commandment without spot or blame until the appearing of our Lord Jesus Christ, which God will bring about in his own time—God, the blessed and only Ruler, the King of kings and Lord of lords, who alone is immortal and who lives in unapproachable light, whom no one has seen or can see. To him be honor and might forever. Amen.*	This is the second formal doxology in First Timothy. It seems that as he grows older Paul's delight at the overwhelming mystery of God has grown deeper. He piles metaphor after metaphor to try to express the wonder he feels at the sheer majesty for his God who has loved him and called him into his service.

Appendix 3 F:
Wish Prayers

Scholars seem to be in agreement that we have no verbatim accounts of Paul's prayers. Rather we have reports about what he prays. It seems to me however, that in the wish-prayers we come very close to hearing Paul pray for those to whom he writes.

Romans 1:8-10

First I thank my God through Jesus Christ for all of you, because your faith is being reported all over the world. God, whom I serve with my whole heart in preaching the gospel of his Son, is my witness how constantly I remember you in my prayers at all times; and I pray that now at last by God's will the way may be opened for me to come to you.

Paul's wish-prayer is that it will be God's will for him to go to Rome and minister there also.

Romans 15:5-6

May the God who gives endurance and encouragement give you a spirit of unity among yourselves as you follow Christ Jesus, so that with one heart and mouth you may glorify the God and Father of our Lord Jesus Christ.

Paul's wish-prayer is that they may be united and glorify God together. He prays that God will give them steadfastness and hopeful cheer and a spirit of oneness in their devotion to Jesus Christ. This will result in their giving glory and praise to God.

Romans 15:13

May the God of hope fill you with all joy and peace as you trust in him, so that you may overflow with hope by the power of the Holy Spirit.

Paul prays that God would pour his Holy Spirit into their lives so that they will have joy and peace and full faith.

2 Corinthians 13:14

May the grace of the Lord Jesus Christ, and the love of God, and the fellowship of the Holy Spirit be with you all.

This benedictory blessing is in the form of a wish prayer. This and Matthew 28:19 are the only places where the triune God is named in a formulary manner.

1 Thessalonians 3:11-13

Now may our God and Father himself and our Lord Jesus clear the way for us to come to you. May the Lord make your love increase and overflow for each other and for everyone else, just as ours does for you. May he strengthen your hearts so that you will be blameless and holy

Paul prays for three things:

1. That our God and Our Lord Jesus would make it possible for him to visit them.
2. That the Lord will cause their love for one another and for Paul to increase and overflow.

in the presence of our God and Father when our Lord Jesus comes with all his holy ones.

3. That God would strengthen their hearts and keep them blameless and holy until Christ returns.

1 Thessalonians 5:23-24
May God himself, the God of peace, sanctify you through and through. May your whole spirit, soul and body be kept blameless at the coming of our Lord Jesus Christ. The one who calls you is faithful and he will do it.

Paul prays that they may experience the peace of God and be made completely holy. He prays that they will be kept blameless in spirit, soul, and body until Christ returns. He ends with the assurance that God is faithful and he will do it.

2 Thessalonians 2:16-17
May the Lord Jesus Christ himself and God our Father, who loved us and by his grace gave us eternal encouragement and good hope, encourage your hearts and strengthen you in every good deed and word.

Paul prays that the Lord Jesus Christ and God our Father would encourage their hearts and strengthen them in every good deed and word. He includes an affirmation of assurance: that God loves them and by his favor and kindness has given us (NB. he includes himself) eternal encouragement and true hope.

2 Thessalonians 3:5
May the Lord direct your hearts into God's love and Christ's perseverance.

Paul prays that their hearts might be focused on God's love and Christ's model of faithful obedience.

2 Thessalonians 3:16
Now may the Lord of peace himself give you peace at all times and in every way. The Lord be with all of you

Paul prays that Christ, who is the Lord of peace give them peace (wholeness, health, assurance) at all times and in every way. He also prays that they might experience the presence of the Lord.

APPENDIX 3 G
THANKS

Romans 1:8-10
First, I thank my God through Jesus Christ for all of you, because your faith is being reported all over the world. God, whom I serve with my whole heart in preaching the gospel of his Son, is my witness how constantly I remember you in my prayers at all times; and I pray that now at last by God's will the way may be opened for me to come to you.

Paul is thankful because of the impact of the reports of the faith of the Roman Christians on the spread of the gospel and the encouragement of Christians in other places.

Romans 1:21-23

For although they knew God, they neither glorified him as God nor gave thanks to him, but their thinking became futile and their foolish hearts were darkened. Although they claimed to be wise, they became fools and exchanged the glory of the immortal God for images...

To refuse to acknowledge God and give thanks to him has dire consequences – it effects how we think and act.

Romans 14:6

He who regards one day as special, does so to the Lord. He who eats meat, eats to the Lord, for he gives thanks to God; and he who abstains, does so to the Lord and gives thanks to God.

This is one of the few places in scripture where a reference is made to praying and giving thanks for our food.

1 Corinthians 1:4-7 *I always thank God for you because of his grace given you in Christ Jesus. For in him you have been enriched in every way--in all your speaking and in all your knowledge--because our testimony about Christ was confirmed in you. Therefore you do not lack any spiritual gift as you eagerly wait for our Lord Jesus Christ to be revealed.*	Because of the grace of God given them in Christ Jesus. They have been enriched in every way in Christ, specifically in speaking and knowledge. This has confirmed Paul's witness to Christ so that they do not lack any spiritual gift and look forward to the coming of Jesus Christ in power.
1 Corinthians 10:29b-30 *For why should my freedom be judged by another's conscience? If I take part in the meal with thankfulness, why am I denounced because of something I thank God for?*	Verse 31 gives the principle involved: *So whether you eat or drink or whatever you do, do it all for the glory of God.*

1 Corinthians 11:23b-24
The Lord Jesus, on the night he was betrayed, took bread, and when he had given thanks, he broke it and said, "This is my body, which is for you; do this in remembrance of me"

Jesus' act of giving thanks before breaking the bread, shows us that we also can give thanks, even in very difficult circumstances.

2 Corinthians 4:15
All this is for your benefit, so that the grace that is reaching more and more people may cause thanksgiving to overflow to the glory of God.

Our faithful endurance in the face of trials can be a testimony to God's grace that causes thanksgiving to overflow to the glory of God.

2 Corinthians 8:16-17
I thank God, who put into the heart of Titus the same concern I have for you. For Titus not only welcomed our appeal, but is coming to you with much enthusiasm and on his own initiative.

Just as Paul rejoices as he sees God at work in Titus just as he works in Paul himself, so our hearts are also encouraged when we see God working in another person's life.

Philippians 1:3-6

I thank my God every time I remember you. In all my prayers for all of you, I always pray with joy because of your partnership in the gospel from the first day until now, being confident of this, that he who began a good work in you will carry it on to completion until the day of Christ Jesus.

He is thankful for their partnership in the gospel which has continued through the years. Paul is thankful for the joy these Philippian Christians have brought him.

Colossians 1:3-6a

We always thank God, the Father of our Lord Jesus Christ, when we pray for you, because we have heard of your faith in Christ Jesus and of the love you have for all the saints-- the faith and love that spring from the hope that is stored up for you in heaven and that you have already heard about in the word of truth, the gospel that has come to you. All over the world this gospel is producing fruit and growing, just as it has been doing among you...

The faith and love with which they responded to the gospel causes Paul to be thankful and rejoice because the fruit of the good news is bearing fruit in them and all over the world.

Colossians 3:15-17

Let the peace of Christ rule in your hearts, since as members of one body you were called to peace. And be thankful. Let the word of Christ dwell in you richly as you teach and admonish one another with all wisdom, and as you sing psalms, hymns and spiritual songs with gratitude in your hearts to God. And whatever you do, whether in word or deed, do it all in the name of the Lord Jesus, giving thanks to God the Father through him.

Gratitude is one of the things that characterize the growing Christian. Whatever we do, we give thanks to God the Father through Christ.

1 Thessalonians 1:2-3

We always thank God for all of you, mentioning you in our prayers. We continually remember before our God and Father your work produced by faith, your labor prompted by love, and your endurance inspired by hope in our Lord Jesus Christ.

Their work *(ergou)* produced by faith. Their labor *(kopou)* prompted by love. Their endurance *(hupomones)* inspired by hope in the Lord Jesus Christ -- causes Paul to thank God for them.

1 Thessalonians 2:13-14

And we also thank God continually because, when you received the word of God, which you heard from us, you accepted it not as the word of men, but as it actually is, the word of God, which is at work in you who believe. For you, brothers, became imitators of God's churches in Judea, which are in Christ Jesus: You suffered from your own countrymen the same things those churches suffered from the Jews,...

They received the word of God from Paul, as it really is, not man's message, but God's word. That word is at work in them and they are standing firm in the face of persecution.

2 Thessalonians 1:3-4

We ought always to thank God for you, brothers, and rightly so, because your faith is growing more and more, and the love every one of you has for each other is increasing. Therefore among God's churches we boast about your perseverance and faith in all the persecutions and trials you are enduring.

Their faith is growing and their love for one another is increasing and they are persevering in the face of persecution and trials.

2 Thessalonians 2:13-14
But we ought always to thank God for you, brothers loved by the Lord, because from the beginning God chose you to be saved through the sanctifying work of the Spirit and through belief in the truth. He called you to this through our gospel, that you might share in the glory of our Lord Jesus Christ.

From the beginning God chose them to be saved through the sanctifying work of the Spirit and belief in the truth.

1 Timothy 1:12-13
I thank Christ Jesus our Lord, who has given me strength, that he considered me faithful, appointing me to his service. Even though I was once a blasphemer and a persecutor and a violent man, I was shown mercy because I acted in ignorance and unbelief. The grace of our Lord was poured out on me abundantly, along with the faith and love that are in Christ Jesus.

Paul gives thanks because Christ has given him strength, considered him faithful and appointed him to his service. In spite of what he had been and done, Paul received mercy and the grace of the Lord was poured out on him abundantly with faith and love that are in Christ Jesus.

2 Timothy 1:3-5

I thank God, whom I serve, as my forefathers did, with a clear conscience, as night and day I constantly remember you in my prayers. Recalling your tears, I long to see you, so that I may be filled with joy. I have been reminded of your sincere faith, which first lived in your grandmother Lois and in your mother Eunice and, I am persuaded, now lives in you also.

Paul thanks God for Timothy and the joy Timothy has brought to him because of his sincere faith which is a part of his heritage from his grandmother and mother.

APPENDIX 3 H: INTERCESSIONS

Romans 10:1-3

Brothers, my heart's desire and prayer to God for the Israelites is that they may be saved. For I can testify about them that they are zealous for God, but their zeal is not based on knowledge. Since they did not know the righteousness that comes from God and sought to establish their own, they did not submit to God's righteousness.

Galatians 4:19-20

My dear children, for whom I am again in the pains of childbirth until Christ is formed in you, how I wish I could be with you now and change my tone, because I am perplexed about you!

Paul's desire and prayer is that the Israelites may be saved and come to a true knowledge of the righteousness of God that comes by faith in Christ and not through our own efforts.

The intensity of his desire for his fellow Jews is graphically stated in Romans 9:2-3 where he writes that he could wish himself to be accursed if that would mean salvation for his countrymen.

Paul's being "*again in the pains of childbirth*, probably refers to the intensity of his concern and prayers on their behalf.

Colossians 2:1-4

I want you to know how much I am struggling for you and for those in Loadicea, and for all who have not met me personally. My purpose is that they may be encouraged in heart and united in love, so that they may have the full riches of complete understanding, in order that they may know the mystery of God, namely, Christ, in whom are hidden all the treasures of wisdom and knowledge.

These verses indicate the intensity of Paul's intercession for these Christians. He also tells them the underlying purpose that draws him to pray for them.

Colossians 4:12

Epaphras, who is one of you and a servant of Christ Jesus, sends greeting. He is always wrestling in prayer for you, that you may stand firm in all the will of God, mature and fully assured.

Epaphras also intercedes with great intensity for his friends in Colosse.

2 Timothy 1:15-18

You know that everyone in the province of Asia has deserted me, including Phygelus and Hermogenes. May the Lord show mercy to the household of Onesiphorus, because he often refreshed me and was not ashamed of any chains. On the contrary, when he as in Rome, he searched hard for me until he found me. May the Lord grant that he will find mercy from the Lord on that day.

Paul prays that the household of Onesiphorus will receive mercy from the Lord because they have deserted him along with many others in the province of Asia. He repeats this request in verse 18.

2 Timothy 4:16-18

At my first defense, no one came to my support, but everyone deserted me. May it not be held against them. But the Lord stood at my side ...

Paul prays that those who had forsaken him at his trial may be forgiven.

Philemon 6-7

I pray that you may be active in sharing your faith, so that you will have a full understanding of every good thing we have in Christ. Your love has given me great joy and encouragement, because you, brother, have refreshed the hearts of the saints.

Literal translation: *that the sharing of your faith may work in (the) knowledge of every good thing for us in Christ.*

NB. The NRSV translates this quite differently: *I pray that the sharing of your faith may promote the knowledge of all the good that is ours in Christ.*

Theme: that the sharing of faith may cause others to understand all the good that is ours in Christ.

NIV: Theme: That as Philemon shares his faith, he may have a full understanding of every good thing we have in Christ.

This verse a good example of why it is impossible to translate from one language to another without there being some interpretation involved.

APPENDIX 3 I
REQUESTS

Romans 15:30-33
I urge you, brothers, by our Lord Jesus Christ and by the love of the Spirit, to join me in my struggle by praying for me. Pray that I may be rescued from the unbelievers in Judea and that my service in Jerusalem may be acceptable to the saints there, so that by God's will I may come to you with joy and together with you be refreshed. The God of peace be with you all. Amen.

When we pray for someone else we are standing with them in their struggle and helping to bear their burden. Here, Paul has three requests:

1. That he would be rescued from the unbelievers.
2. That the Christian's in Jerusalem would accept his service, i.e., the offering he is bringing from the Gentile churches.
3. That he may at last be able to go to Rome and both minister and be ministered to.

Ephesians 6:18-20
And pray in the Spirit on all occasions with all kinds of prayers and requests. With that in mind, be alert and always keep praying for all the saints.

Requests:
That he would be fearless in his proclamation of the gospel and that the words that he speaks will be God's words and not just his.

Pray also for me, that whenever I open my mouth, words may be given me so that I will fearlessly make known the mystery of the gospel, for which I am an ambassador in chains. Pray that I may declare it fearlessly, as I should.

The emphasis he places on "fearlessly" (used twice, v. 19 & 20) indicates the deep apprehension which Paul felt about what lay ahead. Thus his request is that he might be given courage.

Philippians 1:18-20

... *Yes, and I will continue to rejoice, for I know that through your prayers and the help given by the Spirit of Jesus Christ, what has happened to me will turn out for my deliverance. I eagerly expect and hope that I will in no way be ashamed, but will have sufficient courage so that now as always Christ will be exalted in my body, whether by life or by death.*

Paul is so certain of the prayers and support of his friends in Philippi that he makes his request for their prayers almost in the form of a "thank you." He is sure that through their prayers and the help given by the Holy Spirit, the difficult situation he is in will result in his release from prison. He indicates his need for courage and boldness so that he will be able to clearly glorify Christ, no matter what happens.

Colossians 4:2-4
Devote yourselves to prayer, being watchful and thankful. And pray for us, too, that God may open a door for our message, so that we may proclaim the mystery of Christ, for which I am in chains. Pray that I may proclaim it clearly, as I should.

Paul requests prayer that he might be able to take advantage of the opportunity to proclaim the gospel of Christ. He specifically asks that they pray for him to be able to proclaim the gospel with clarity.

Colossians 4:18
I, Paul, write this greeting in my own hand. Remember my chains. Grace be with you.

Remember my chains means pray for my release from prison.

1 Thessalonians 5:25
Brothers, pray for us.

Paul deeply values the prayers of others.

2 Thessalonians 3:1-2
Finally, brothers, pray for us that the message of the Lord May spread rapidly and be honored, just as it was with you. And pray that we may be delivered from wicked and evil men, for not everyone has faith.

Paul's request is that the gospel of Christ might be accepted so that the number of believers would quickly grow. He also asks them to pray for his safety and protection from those who oppose the gospel

APPENDIX 3 J: GENERAL/MISC.

Romans 5:11

Not only is this so, but we also rejoice in God through our Lord Jesus Christ, through whom we have now received reconciliation.

"We Rejoice in God through our Lord Jesus Christ." This is prayer language.

Romans 10:13-15

For, "Everyone who calls on the name of the Lord will be saved." How, then, can they call on the one they have not believed in? And how can they believe in the one of whom they have not heard? And how can they hear without someone preaching to them? And how can they preach unless they are sent? ...

To call on the name of the Lord is prayer. These verses show that there is preparation if true prayer is to be prayed.

The preparation here is hearing and believing.

1 Corinthians 7:5

Do not deprive each other except by mutual consent and for a time, so that you may devote yourselves to prayer. Then come together again so that Satan will not tempt you because of your lack of self-control.

Devoting oneself to prayer may demand a temporary change of life-style.

1 Corinthians 16:22

If anyone does not love the Lord—a curse be on him. Come, O Lord! (Maran tha)

Is a curse a prayer?

Maran tha = a prayer for the return of Christ.

2 Corinthians 9:11-15

You will be made rich in every way so that you can be generous on every occasion, and through us your generosity will result in thanksgiving to God. This service that you perform is not only supplying the needs of God's people but is also overflowing in may expressions of thanks to God. Because of the service by which you have proved yourselves, men will praise God for the obedience that

There are a number of references to prayer in this passage which show that the most natural thing in the world is for a follower of Christ to pray with many different kinds of prayer.

accompanies your confession of the gospel of Christ, and for your generosity in sharing with them and with everyone else. And in their prayers for you their hearts will go out to you, because of the surpassing grace God has given you. Thanks be to God for his indescribable gift.

2 Corinthians 12:7-9

...there was given me a thorn in the flesh, a messenger of Satan, to torment me. Three times I pleaded with the Lord to take it away from me. But he said to me, "My grace is sufficient for you, for may power is made perfect in weakness." Therefore I will boast all the more gladly about my weaknesses, so that Christ's power may rest on me.

Not every prayer is answered as we would like. But God gives his assurance and grace that he will use our distress to display his power. It demands humility and submission if we are to be the instruments of grace that bring God's presence and power into a situation.

2 Corinthians 13:7

Now we pray to God that you will not do anything wrong. Not that people will see that we have stood the test but that you will do what is right even though we may seem to have failed..

This is a very general intercessory prayer, and shows that our concerns are a natural call for us to pray.

2 Timothy 2:22

Flee the evil desires of youth, and pursue righteousness, faith, love and peace, along with those who call on the Lord out of a pure heart.

Moral purity and the pursuit of a holy life unites us with others who are praying out of a pure heart. Jesus said that it is the pure in heart who will see God (Matt. 5:8). Again we have the importance of preparation if our prayers are to be effective.

Philemon 22

And one thing more: Prepare a guest room for me, because I hope to be restored to you in answer to your prayers.

Paul believed the prayers of others on his behalf made a difference and that his hoped for release from prison would be an answer to Philemon's prayer for him.

END NOTES

Paul began his Christian life in prayer

1) See appendix II which lists all the references to prayer in Paul's letters. There are 105 passages (many of which are several verses long) spread through the 87 chapters that comprise his 13 letters. Although many scholars question and reject the Pauline authorship of Ephesians, Colossians, 1 & 2 Timothy, and Titus, in this study I have treated them all as coming from the pen of the Apostle.

2) The practice of praying 3 times a day was widespread in Judaism at the time of Christ. The practice was based on Psalm 55:16-17, "But I call to God, and the LORD saves me. Evening, morning and noon I cry out in distress, and he hears my voice." Daniel 6:10 affirms the practice, "…three times a day he got down on his knees and prayed, giving thanks to God, just as he had done before."

Jesus described well the Pharisaic practice of piety in the parable given in Luke 18:9-14. "*The Pharisee stood up and prayed about himself: 'God, I thank you that I am not like all other men--robbers, evildoers, adulterers--or even like this tax collector. I fast twice a week and give a tenth of all I get*" (vv.11-12).

3) In an article "Prayer in the Pauline Letters" in Richard Longnecker, ed. *Into God's Presence: Prayer in the New Testament,* Grand Rapids, Eerdmans Publ. Co., 2001.

4) The Eighteen Benediction are known as the *Shmoneh* Esrai, or the Amidah.

The Amidah Prayer: A New Translation
By David Bivin

Since the prayer Jesus taught his disciples (The Lord's Prayer) is apparently an abbreviated version of the Amidah ("Standing," in Hebrew) or Eighteen Benedictions, I think it is important for Christians to be familiar with this central prayer of Jewish life. The prayer is very ancient, some of the changes to it being made 200 years before the time of Jesus. The prayer is also very beautiful, full of scriptural quotations and allusions. Every Jew was obligated to pray the Eighteen Benedictions daily; however, in times of emergency, one was permitted to pray a shortened form of the Eighteen, such as the Lord's Prayer.

Rabbi Eliezer, a younger contemporary of Jesus, taught this abbreviation of the Eighteen: "May your will be done in heaven above, grant peace of mind to those who fear you [on earth] below, and do what seems best to you. Blessed are you, O LORD, who answers prayer." Note the phrases "Your will be done" and "in heaven above…[on earth] below" as in the Lord's Prayer. Also note the parallel between "grant peace of mind" in the prayer Eliezer taught and "deliver us from evil" in the prayer Jesus taught.

The headings in capital letters (e.g., "THE GOD OF HISTORY") that summarize each benediction or blessing are for reference only, and are not to be recited. The characterizations of God, which always follow "Blessed are you, O Lord", also can be used to summarize each benediction, and , if strung together, comprise a nice description of God: God is the shield of Abraham, the one who revives the dead, the holy God, the gracious giver of knowledge, the one who delights in repentance, the one who is merciful and always ready to forgive, the redeemer of Israel, the healer of Israel's sick, the one who blesses the years, the one who gathers Israel's dispersed, the King who loves righteousness and justice, the one who smashes enemies and humbles the arrogant, the support and stay of the righteous, the one who hears prayer, the one who rebuilds Jerusalem, the one who causes salvation to flourish, the one who hears prayer, the one who restores the divine presence to Zion, the one whose name is the

Beneficient One and to whom it is fitting to give thanks, and the one who blesses Israel with peace.

THE AMIDAH

1. THE GOD OF HISTORY:

Blessed are you, O Lord our God and God of our fathers, the God of Abraham, the God of Isaac and the God of Jacob, the great, mighty and revered God, the Most High God who bestows lovingkindnesses, the creator of all things, who remembers the good deeds of the patriarchs and in love will bring a redeemer to their children's children for his name's sake. O king, helper, savior and shield.

Blessed are you, O Lord, the shield of Abraham.

2. THE GOD OF NATURE:

You, O Lord, are mighty forever, you revive the dead, you have power to save. [From the end of Sukkot until the evening of Passover, insert: You cause the wind to blow and the rain to fall.] You sustain the living with lovingkindness, you revive the dead with great mercy, you support the falling, heal the sick, set free the bound and keep faith with those who sleep in the dust. Who is like you, O doer of mighty acts? Who resembles you, a king who puts to death and restores to life, and causes salvation to flourish? And you are certain to revive the dead.

Blessed are you, O Lord, who revives the dead.

3. SANCTIFICATION OF GOD:

[Reader] We will sanctify your name in this world just as it is sanctified in the hightest heavens, as it is written by your prophet: "And they call out to one another and say:

[Cong.] 'Holy, holy, holy is the LORD of hosts; the whole earth is full of his glory.' " [Isa. 6:3]

[Reader] Those facing them praise God saying:

[Cong.] "Blessed be the Presence of the LORD in his place." [Ezek. 3:12]

[Reader] And in your Holy Words if is written, saying,

[Cong] "The LORD reigns forever, your God, O Zion, throughout all generations. Hallelujah." [Ps. 146:10]

[Reader] Throughout all generations we will declare your greatness, and to all eternity we will proclaim your holiness. Your praise, O our God, shall never depart from our mouth, for you are a great and holy God and King. Blessed are you, O Lord, the holy God. You are holy, and your name is holy, and holy beings praise you daily. (Selah.) Blessed are you, O Lord, the holy God.

4. PRAYER FOR UNDERSTANDING:

You favor men with knowledge, and teach mortals understanding. O favor us with the knowledge, the understanding and the insight that come from you.

Blessed are you, O Lord, the gracious giver of knowledge.

5. FOR REPENTANCE:

Bring us back, O our Father, to your Instruction; draw us near, O our King, to your service; and cause us to return to you in perfect repentance. Blessed are you, O Lord, who delights in repentance.

6. FOR FORGIVENESS:

Forgive us, O our Father, for we have sinned; pardon us, O our King, for we have transgressed; for you pardon and forgive. Blessed are you, O Lord, who is merciful and always ready to forgive.

7. FOR DELIVERANCE FROM AFFLICTION:

Look upon our affliction and plead our cause, and redeem us speedily for your name's sake, for you are a mighty redeemer. Blessed are you, O Lord, the redeemer of Israel.

8. FOR HEALING:

Heal us, O Lord, and we will be healed; save us and we will be saved, for you are our praise. O grant a perfect healing to all our ailments, for you, almighty King, are a faithful and merciful healer. Blessed are you, O Lord, the healer of the sick of his people Israel.

9. FOR DELIVERANCE FROM WANT:

Bless this year for us, O Lord our God, together with all the varieties of its produce, for our welfare. Bestow ([from the 15th of Nissan insert:] dew and rain) for a blessing upon the face of the earth. O satisfy us with your goodness, and bless our year like the best of years. Blessed are you, O Lord, who blesses the years.

10. FOR GATHERING OF EXILES:

Sound the great shofar for our freedom, raise the ensign to gather our exiles, and gather us from the four corners of the earth. Blessed are you, O Lord, who gathers the dispersed of his people Israel.

11. FOR THE RIGHTEOUS REIGN OF GOD:

Restore our judges as in former times, and our counselors as at the beginning; and remove from us sorrow and sighing. Reign over us, you alone, O Lord, with lovingkindness and compassion,, and clear us in judgment. Blessed are you, O Lord, the King who loves righteousness and justice.

12. FOR THE DESTRUCTION OF APOSTATES AND THE ENEMIES OF GOD:

Let there be no hope for slanderers, and let all wickedness perish in an instant. May all your enemies quickly be cut down, and may you soon in our day uproot, crush, cast down and humble the dominion of arrogance. Blessed are you, O Lord, who smashes enemies and humbles the arrogant.

13. FOR THE RIGHTEOUS AND PROSELYTES:

May your compassion be stirred, O Lord our God, towards the righteous, the pious, the elders of your people the house of Israel, the remnant of their scholars, towards proselytes, and towards us also. Grant a good reward to all who truly trust in your name. Set our lot with them forever so that we may never be put to shame, for we have put our trust in you. Blessed are you, O Lord, the support and stay of the righteous.

14. FOR THE REBUILDING OF JERUSALEM:

Return in mercy Jerusalem your city, and dwell in it as you have promised. Rebuild it soon in our day as an eternal structure, and quickly set up in it the throne of David. Blessed are you, O Lord, who rebuilds Jerusalem.

15, FOR THE MESSIANIC KING:

Speedily cause the offspring of your servant David to flourish, and let him be exalted by your saving power, for we wait all day long for your salvation. Blessed are you, O Lord, who causes salvation to flourish.

16. FOR THE ANSWERING OF PRAYER:

Hear our voice, O Lord our God; spare us and have pity on us. Accept our prayer in mercy and with favor, for you are a God who hears prayers and supplications. O our King, do not turn us away from your presence empty-handed, for you hear the prayers of your people Israel with compassion. Blessed are you, O Lord, who hears prayer.

17. FOR RESTORATION OF TEMPLE SERVICE:

Be pleased, O Lord our God, with your people Israel and with their prayers. Restore the service to the inner sanctuary of your Temple, and receive in love and with favor both the fire-offerings of Israel and their prayers, May the worship of your people Israel always be acceptable to you. And let our eyes behold your return in mercy to Zion. Blessed are you, O Lord, who restores his divine presence to Zion.

18. THANKSGIVING FOR GOD'S UNFAILINHG MERCIES:

We give thanks to you that you are the Lord our God and the God of our fathers forever and ever. Through every generation you have been the rock of our lives, the shield of our salvation. We will give you thanks and declare your praise for our lives that are committed into your hands, for our souls that are entrusted to you, for your miracles that are daily with us, and with peace.

*The prayer is known as the "Eighteen" because it originally consisted of eighteen benedictions. See David Bivin, "Prayers for Emergencies," Jerusalem Perspective-37 (Mar./Apr. 1992), pp. 16-17.

This article is from a free monthly "Pipeline" email available from Jerusalem Perspective.

PART ONE: PAUL'S PRACTICE OF PRAYER

5) In Hebrews through Jude there are only two prayers, Heb. 13:20-21 and Jude 24-25. Both of these are a doxological benediction and blessing. In Revelations there are several doxologies, but no prayers for the recipients of the document. There are no prayers in James, 1 & 2 Peter, 1, 2, 3 John.

6) Four such books are: Donald Coggan, *The Prayers of the New Testament,* London, Hodder and Stoughton, 1967; Ray Pritchard, *Beyond all you could ask or think: how to pray like the Apostle Paul,* Chicago, Moody Publishers, 2004; D.A. Carson, *A Call to Spiritual Reformation: Priorities from Paul and His Prayers,* Grand Rapids, Baker Books and Inter-Varsity Press, 1992; David Bordon with Rick Killian, *Discover the Power in the Prayers of Paul*, Tulsa, Harrison House Publishers, 2005.

7) The unity of the church is mentioned in most of Paul's letters, i.e., Romans 14 & 15; 1 Corinthians 1:10; 12; Galatians 5:13-16, 26; Ephesians 2:11-22, 4:1-16; Philippians 2:1-4; Colossians 3:12-17; 1 Thessalonians 3:11-13, 4:9-10; 2 Thessalonians 1:3.

8) Some of the metaphors for the church which Paul uses are: Church (*ecclesia*) - the people of God gathered for worship; body of Christ; family of God; household of God; the Israel of God; temple of God; bride of Christ; people of God. See Paul Minear, *Images of the Church in the New Testament,* Philadelphia, Westminster Press 1960 and most books on Paul's Theology.

9) Other expressions of this concern are: Acts 20:31; Romans 1:11; 2 Corinthians 2:4, 11; 7:12; 12:20-21; Galatians 4:11, 19; and 1 Thessalonians 3:10.

10) See Colossians 1:28-29; Galatians 4:19; and Ephesians 4:11-13. I

11) Thessalonians 2:19-20. See also 2 Corinthians 3:2-3; Philippians 2:14-16.

12) Norman Grubb, Rees Howells Intercessor, Fort Washington, PA, 1952 (2002 edition), p. 110. It may be helpful to set this quotation in context. Howells was interceding for orphans and he writes: "…one can pray continually for the orphans and ask the Lord to be a Father to them, even through others, because one only asks Him to do through another what he is willing for the Lord to do through him. This is the law of intercession on every level of life that only so far as we have been tested and proved willing to do a thing ourselves can we intercede for others. Christ is our Intercessor because He took the place of each one prayed for.

We are never called to intercede for sin; that has been done once and for all. But we are often called to intercede for sinners and their needs, and the Holy Ghost can never 'bind the strong man' through us on a higher level than that in which He has first had victory in us." pp. 109-110.

In an earlier passage Norman Grubbs writes about Christ's intercession. "Perhaps believers in general have regarded intercession as just some form of rather intensified prayer. It is, so long as there is great emphasis on the word 'intensified'; for there are three things to be seen in an intercessor which are not necessarily found in ordinary prayer: identification, agony and authority.

The identification of the intercessor with the ones for whom he intercedes is perfectly seen in the Savior. Of Him it was said that He poured out His soul unto death; and was numbered with the transgressors; and He bare the sin of many, and *made intercession for* the transgressors. As the Divine Intercessor, interceding for a lost world, He drained the cup of our lost condition to its last drop, He 'tasted death for every man.' To do that, in the fullest possible sense, He sat where we sit. By taking our nature upon Himself, by learning obedience through the things which He suffered, by being poor for our sakes, and finally by being made sin for us, He gained the position in which, with the fullest authority as the Captain of our salvation made perfect through sufferings, and fullest understanding of all we go through, He can ever live to make intercession for us, and by effective pleadings with the Father 'is able to save to the uttermost them that come unto God by Him.' Identification is thus the first law of the intercessor. He pleads effectively because he gives his life for those he pleads for; he is their genuine representative; he has submerged his self-interest in their needs and sufferings, and as far as possible has literally taken their place. *ibid.* p. 94.

Oswald Cambers, in his book *If Ye Shall Ask...* p. 93. Has these comments to make about intercession.

"Prayer is simple, prayer is supernatural, and to anyone not related to our Lord Jesus Christ, prayer is apt to look stupid. It does sound unreasonable to say that God will do things in answer to prayer, yet our Lord said that He would. Our Lord bases everything on prayer, then the key to all our work as Christians is, 'Pray ye therefore (Matthew 9:38).

When we pray for others the Spirit of God works in the unconscious domain of their being that we know nothing about, and the one we are praying for knows nothing about, but after the passing of time the conscious life of the one prayed for begins to show signs of unrest and disquiet. We may have spoken until we are worn out, but have never come anywhere near, and we have given up in despair. But if we have been praying, we find on meeting them one day that there is the beginning of a softening in an enquiry and a desire to know something. It is that kind of intercession that does most damage to Satan's kingdom. It is slight, so feeble in its initial stages that if reason is not wedded to the light of the Holy Spirit, we will never obey it, and yet it is that kind of intercession that the New Testament places most emphasis on, though it has so little to show for it. It seems stupid to think that we can pray and all that will happen, but remember to whom we pray, we pray to a God who understands the unconscious depths of personality about which we know nothing, and He has told us to pray. The great Master of the human heart said, 'Greater works than these shall he do…And whatsoever ye shall ask in my name, that will I do.' "

13) My friend Dr. Oliver Blosser observed that "the promise of grace came after Paul's third prayer. In Hebrew thought, the number three refers

to completeness/perfection. The LORD always does something supernatural on the third day or after the third time."

14) Daniel Henderson, *Fresh Encounters, NAVPRESS, Colorado Springs, Co., 2004. p. 85.*

15) Oswald Chambers, *My Utmost For His Highest, April 26.*

16) Oswald Chambers, *The Place of Help,* p. 34

17) Oswald Chambers, *The Servant as His Lord.* p. 121

18) This end note focuses primarily on the physical sufferings.

1 Corinthians 4:9-13. *For it seems to me that God has put us apostles on display at the end of the procession, like men condemned to death. We have become a spectacle for the world, for angels, and for people to stare at. We are fools for Christ's sake, but you are wise in Christ. We are weak, but you are strong. You are honored, but we are dishonored. To this very hour we are hungry, thirsty, dressed in rags, brutally treated, and homeless. We wear ourselves out from working with our own hands. When insulted, we bless. When persecuted, we endure. When slandered, we answer with kind words. Up to this moment we have become the filth of the world, the scum of the universe!*

2 Corinthians 4:7-10 *But we have this treasure in clay jars to show that its extraordinary power comes from God and not from us. In every way we are troubled but not crushed, frustrated but not in despair, persecuted but not abandoned, struck down but not destroyed. We are always carrying around the death of Jesus in our bodies, so that the life of Jesus may be clearly shown in our bodies. While we are alive, we are constantly being handed over to death for Jesus' sake, so that the life of Jesus may be clearly shown in our dying bodies.*

2 Corinthians 6:4-10 *Instead, in every way we demonstrate that we are God's servants by tremendous endurance in the midst of difficulties,* *hardships, and calamities; in beatings, imprisonments, and riots; in hard work, sleepless nights, and hunger; with purity, knowledge, patience, and kindness; with the Holy Spirit, genuine love, truthful speech, and divine power; through the weapons of righteousness in the right and left hands; through honor and dishonor; through ill repute and good repute; perceived as deceivers and yet true, as unknown and yet well-known, as dying and yet—as you see—very much alive, as punished and yet not killed, as sorrowful and yet always rejoicing, as poor and yet enriching many, as having nothing and yet possessing everything.*

2 Corinthians 7:5 *For even when we came to Macedonia, our bodies had no rest. We suffered in a number of ways. Outwardly there were conflicts, inwardly there were fears.*

2 Corinthians 11:21-29 *Whatever anyone else dares to claim—I am talking like a fool—I can claim it, too. Are they Hebrews? So am I. Are they Israelites? So am I. Are they Abraham's descendants? So am I. Are they Christ's servants? I am insane to talk like this, but I am a far better one! I have been involved in far greater efforts, far more imprisonments, countless beatings, and have faced death more than once. Five times I received from the Jews forty lashes minus one. Three times I was beaten with a stick, once I was pelted with stones, three times I was shipwrecked, and I drifted on the sea for a day and a night. I have been involved in frequent journeys, in dangers from rivers, dangers from robbers, dangers from my own people, dangers from the Gentiles, dangers in the city, dangers in the open country, dangers at sea, dangers from false brothers, in toil and hardship, through many a sleepless night, through hunger and thirst, through many periods of fasting, through coldness and nakedness. Besides everything else, I have a daily burden because of my anxiety about all the churches. Who is weak without me being weak, too? Who is caused to stumble without me becoming indignant?*

For a more complete list of Paul's sufferings that includes emotional and spiritual suffering, I refer you to the appendix.

19) It is probably significant that in his first two missionary journeys Paul is accompanied by men who were highly respected by the Jerusalem church. The Christians in Jerusalem never trusted Paul (when he was arrested it seems the whole church abandoned him and there is no mention of any help being given him) and so he was careful to have men with him they did trust in order to affirm his ministry. There is no mention of such a companion on his third missionary journey.

20) 1 Corinthians 11:1; 4:16; Phil. 3:17, 4:19; 2 Thess. 3:7. For being worthy: Ephesians 4:1; Colossians 1:10; 1 Thessalonians 2:12; 2 Thessalonians 1:11.

21) Verlyn D. Verbugge, *The NIV Theological Dictionary of New Testament Words.* Grand Rapids, Zondervan Publishing House, 2000. p. 846.

22) The Greek word translated "without ceasing" in classical Greek is used to refer to a "hacking cough."

PART TWO: PAUL'S TEACHING ON PRAYER Section I
The Holy Spirit and Prayer

23) I am indebted to Arthur Wallis' book, *Pray in the Spirit: The Work of the Holy Spirit in the Ministry of Prayer,* Eastbourne, G.B., Kingsway Publications, 1970, for many of the insights on the subject of the Holy Spirit and Prayer.

24) The only other writer to connect the Holy Spirit with prayer is the phrase in Jude 20, "pray in the Spirit."

25) It occurs only here and in Luke 10:40 -- the story of Mary and Martha in which Martha asks Jesus to tell Mary to "help her."

26) Paul's warning to the Corinthians is worth noting: *So, if you think you are standing firm, be careful that you don't fall* (1 Corinthians 10:12).

27) Oswald Chambers, *Biblical Ethics, p. 51.*

28) Romans 12:1, *Therefore, I urge you, brothers, in view of God's mercy, to offer your bodies as living sacrifices, holy and pleasing to God--which is your spiritual worship.*

29) C. S. Lovett, *Dealing with the Devil* , Baldwin Park, CA, Personal Christianity, 1967.

30) Oswald Chambers, *My Utmost... June 23*

31) Proverbs 3:5-6 tells us four things: 1. A command: Trust in the Lord; 2. A warning: Do not lean on your own understanding; 3. How to heed the warning: In all you ways acknowledge God 4. A promise: and he will direct your paths.

32) See the commentaries on Romans by Dunn, Cranfield, and Nyggren; see also J.D.G. Dunn, Jesus and the Spirit, Philadelphia, Westminster Press, 1975, pp. 312-318.

33) James Hawkinson , *Glad Hearts The Joys of Believing and Challenges of Belonging*, Chicago, Il., Covenant Publications, 2003, p. 1.

34) Paul Billheimer, in his book *Destined for the Throne* , Fort Washington, PA, Christian Literature Crusade, 1975, P. 48.

35) Henri Nouwen, *The Wounded Healer, Ministry in Contemporary Society,* Garden City, NY, Image Books, Doubleday & Company Inc.

36) Quoted in Hawkinson, *Glad Hearts,* p.46

37) Robert Robinson, "Come Thou Fount of Every Blessing"

38) C. O. Rosinius, *Commentary on Romans.* Quoted by Hawkinson, Glad Hearts, p.13.

39) See the commentaries on Romans by J.D.G. Dunn, C.E.B. Cranfield, Nygren, etc. Calvin understands this verse as referring to "spiritual resurrection."

40) L.B. Cowman, edited by James Reimann, STREAMS IN THE DESERT, Grand Rapids, MI, Zondervan, 1997. May 13, pp. 192-193.

41) Arthur Wallis, *Pray in the Spirit: The Work of the Holy Spirit in the Ministry of Prayer,* Eastbourne, G.B., Kingsway Publications, 1970, pp.24-26.

42) ibid. p. 26.

43) This lecture was revised and printed in Ray S. Anderson, ed., *Theological Foundations for Ministry,* Grand Rapids, Wm. B. Eerdmans Publishing Company, 1979, pp. 302-369

Paul's Teaching on Prayer: Section II

44) John 14:13-14; 15:7, 16; 16:24.

45) Charles Hodge writes: We have "free and unrestricted access to God, as children to a father. We come with the assurance of being accepted, because our confidence does not rest on our own merit, but on the infinite merit of an infinite Saviour. It is *in him* we have this liberty. We have this free access to God; we believers; not any particular class, a priesthood among Christians to whom alone access is permitted, but all believers without any priestly intervention, other than that of one great High Priest who has passed through the heavens, Jesus the Son of God." The word translated "freedom" "as used in Scripture, is not merely *freespokenness,* nor yet simple *frankness,* but *fearlessness,* freedom from apprehension of rejection or of evil. It is this Christ has procured for us. Even the vilest may, in Christ, approach the infinitely holy, who is a consuming fire, with fearlessness. Nothing short of an infinite Saviour could effect such a redemption." After writing about the phrase *through faith in him*, Hodge

makes this point: "It is the dignity of his person, confidence in the efficacy of his blood, and assurance of his love, all of which are included, more or less consciously, in faith, that enables us joyfully to draw near to God. This is the great question which every sinner needs to have answered--How may I come to God with the assurance of acceptance? The answer given by the apostle and confirmed by the experience of the saints of all ages is, 'by faith in Jesus Christ' "

Charles Hodge, An Exposition of Ephesians, Wilmington, Delaware, Associated Publishers and Authors Inc., no date. Pp. 61-62.

46) Other references to Christ as our mediator are: Hebrews 9:15, 24; 12:24; 1 John 2:1 and Romans 8:34.

47) Oswald Chambers, My Utmost for his Highest, July 16.

48) The only posture which Paul mentions is kneeling (Ephesians 3:14) which indicates humility and submission.

49) In this number I have included only two of Paul's requests for prayer for himself.

50) The concept of binding is found in Matthew 16:19 and 18:18 and implied elsewhere in the New Testament.

51) For a discussion of 1 Corinthians 14 and praying in tongues see the discussion in the section "Paul Prayed in Tongues."

PART THREE: A FRESH LOOK AT THE SALUTATIONS
The Apostolic Blessing

52) If 1 Thessalonians is the first letter that Paul wrote, as many scholars believe, then we have evidence of development in the way he begins his letters; not with a greeting from himself but with a blessing from God the Father and the Lord Jesus Christ.

53) Paul's letters are specifically referred to by Peter (2 Peter 3:15), and John ministered in the vicinity of Ephesus and would thus be acquainted with Paul's correspondence to Ephesus, Colosse, and Loadicia. Hebrews, 1 & 3 John do not have a greeting.

54) Gallagher and Hawthorne in their article in a section titled: "What Does "Blessing" Mean" wrote: If our only source were the book of Genesis, we would learn a great deal about the idea of blessing. In Genesis, the word "blessing" is used in two distinct ways. First, we see the term blessing used to describe a pronouncement or endowment of blessing. It is an act in which a future destiny or goodness is spoken, and thus bestowed upon the person or entity being blessed. Second, the term blessing is used to describe the fulfillment of what was promised, whether material or otherwise. The word blessing, then, refers both to the giving of blessing as well as to the gifts that blessing brings forth. P.34.

In a section called "Blessing as Endowment" the authors write:

Throughout the rest of Scripture the idea of blessing remains linked to the idea of life flourishing toward an intended fullness. When blessing is fulfilled in creatures, people, households or nations, they are enabled to move toward their intended destiny. That change may be slow or rapid. Blessing is never seen as magical, but rather a dynamic of God's life.

Further on in the record of Genesis, we see more occasions in which words of blessing are pronounced. Jacob's struggle with Esau to obtain his father's pronouncement of blessing is the most prominent instance (Gen 27). His struggle with an angel (or with God?) to obtain a pronouncement of blessing is noteworthy: "I will not let go unless you bless me." (32:26-

29), In every case, this verbal giving of blessing was understood as far more than words, but as an irrevocable transfer of God's special enablement and abundance. Sarita D. Gallagher and Steven C. Hawthorne. "Blessing as Transformation" in *PERSPECTIVES on the World Christian Movement.* A Reader, Fourth Edition. Editors: Ralph D. Winter and Steven C. Hawthorne. William Carey Library, Pasadena, CA, 2009 pp. 34,35.

55) Some modern translations, like the NTLB, turn the greeting into a wish prayer. Now Paul has many wish prayers in his letters (see the list in the appendix). And in a sense there may not be a lot of distinction to be made between the salutation as a blessing and as a wish-prayer. The point I am making is that there is a regular grammatical form for expressing a wish which the salutations do not fit.

56) Richard Bauckham gives some wonderful perspective on the Abrahamic blessing: "Blessing is a rich Biblical notion that has been rather neglected in our theology. Blessing in the Bible refers to God's characteristically generous and abundant giving of all good to his creatures and his continual renewal of the abundance of created life. Blessing is God's provision for human flourishing. But it is also relational: to be blessed by God's good gifts is not only to know God's good gifts but to know God himself in his generous giving. Because blessing is relational, the movement of the blessing is a movement that goes out from God and returns to him. God's blessing of people overflows in their blessing of others, and, those who experience blessing from God in turn bless God, which means that they give all that creatures really can give to God: thanksgiving and praise.

"Blessing highlights the relationship between creation and salvation in a different way from other ways of characterizing God's activity in the world. Already on the fifth day of creation God blesses (Gen 1:22). Blessing is the way God enables his creation to be fertile and fruitful, to grow and to flourish. It is in the most comprehensive sense God's purpose for his creation. Wherever human life enjoys the good things of creation and produces the good fruits of human activity, God is pouring out his blessing. Wherever people bless God for his blessings, to that extent God is known as the good Creator who provides for human flourishing. God's blessing is universal.

"But we should not think of the idea of blessing as something that describes God's goodness in creation, but does not also help us understand his goodness in salvation. Salvation too is God's blessing, since salvation is the fulfillment of God's purposes in spite of the damage evil does to God's creation. The Abrahamic blessing is more than the blessing of creation because it is designed to contend with and to overcome its opposite: God's curse.

"With sin God's curse enters creation alongside of God's blessing. We found the universal background to God's promise to Abraham in the account of the nations in Genesis 10-11. But there is an even earlier background in Genesis 3-4, where the blessings of creation turn to curse (3:17; 4:11). The curse even enters into God's promise to Abraham, apparently paralleling the blessing. God says to Abraham in Genesis 12: "I will bless those who bless you and the one who curses you I will curse" (Gen 12:3; cf. 27:29; Num 24:9). But blessing predominates in the promise (as the difference between the plural "those who bless you" and the singular "the one who curses you" seems to suggest), and it is clearly blessing, not curse that is the goal of God's calling of Abraham. Therefore blessing has the last word in the promise: "in you all the families of the earth shall be blessed."

"Through the story of Israel curse continually accompanies blessing (e.g., Deut 7:12-16; 27-28), but the ultimate goal of God's promise to Abraham is the blessing that will prevail over the curse. It does when the seed of Abraham, the singled-out descendant of Abraham, the Messiah, becomes "a curse for us…so that in Christ Jesus the blessing of Abraham might come to the Gentiles" (Gal 3:13-14). This is why God's promise that the nations will be blessed is called "the gospel" by Paul (Gal 3:8). The secret of the promise is Christ's bearing of the curse so that the blessing may prevail. The gospel is that in Jesus Christ the curse has been set aside and God's creative purpose for the blessing of his creation is established beyond any possibility of reversal. God's last and effective word is his blessing. It is a particular word, spoken in the life, death and resurrection of Jesus, broadcast by those who like Paul cannot but pass it on, so powerful is its effect, overflowing with blessing from those who, blessed by it, become a blessing to others."

Richard Bauckham, *Bible and Mission,* 2003, Grand Rapids, MI, Backer Academic Books. Taken from *PERSPECTIVES on the World Christian Movement.* A Reader, Fourth Edition. Editors: Ralph D. Winter and Steven C. Hawthorne. William Carey Library, Pasadena, CA, 2009 pp. 38-39.

57) I owe the number and the insight that the covenant had two principle parts which were often repeated in an abridged and paraphrased form to Don Richardson in a lecture I heard him give to the Covenant Minister's Midwinter Conference in 1996.

58) Allow me to give four short statements from Oswald Chambers. "The great characteristic of Paul's life was that he realized he was not his own: he had been bought with a price, and he never forgot it…

'I have become all things to all men, that I might by all possible means save some.' (1 Corinthians 9:22). Paul attracted to Jesus all the time, never to himself. He became a sacramental personality, that is, wherever he went Jesus Christ helped Himself to his life." Chambers; *So Send I You*, pp 21-23

In 2 Corinthians 2:14 Paul states this: *But thanks be to God, who always leads us in triumphal procession in Christ and through us spreads everywhere the fragrance of the knowledge of him.* See also 2 Corinthians 1:3-5.

"To be a sacramental personality means that the elements of the natural life are presented by God as they are broken providentially in His service. We have to be adjusted into God before we can be broken bread in His hands. Keep right with God and let Him do what He likes, and you will find that He is producing the kind of bread and wine that will benefit His other children." *My Utmost…S*eptember 30

"God rarely allows a soul to see how great a blessing he is…If you believe in Jesus, you will find that God has nourished in you mighty torrents of blessing for others." Chambers, *My Utmost…* Sept. 6

"...others are stronger and better for knowing you... There are some people in whose company you cannot have a mean thought without being instantly rebuked." Chambers, *The place of Help,* p. 79.

59) Eugene H. Peterson, *The Power of a Blessing*, Colorado Springs, CO. Navpress, 2004. Pp. 7-11. See also Bill Gothard, *The Power of Spoken Blessings,* Sisters OR, Multnomah Press, 2004.

A New Understanding of Salvation

60) William Barclay says this about *charis*, the Greek word translated "grace": *"Charis* is a lovely word: the basic ideas in it are joy and pleasure, brightness and beauty; It is in fact, connected with the English word *charm*. But with Jesus Christ there comes a new beauty to add to the beauty that was there. And that beauty is born of a new relationship to God--the relationship of *grace*. With Christ life becomes lovely because man is no longer the victim of the law of God; he has become the child of the love of God. With Christ there comes the supreme beauty of discovering God the Father." William Barclay, Colossians , Daily Study Bible

61) Oswald Chambers, *My Utmost for His Highest*, November 28.

62) Max Lucado, *Just Like Jesus*. Nashville: Word Publishing, 1998. Pp. 145-146.

63) James D. G. Dunn, *The Theology of Paul the Apostle,* Grand Rapids: William B. Eerdmans Publishing Co., 1998; pp. 328-333. The quotation is pp. 331-332.

64) Cornelius Plantinga, Jr., *Not the Way Its Supposed to Be,* William B. Eerdmans Publishing Co., 1996, p. 14.

65) see footnote #4

A New Understanding of God: God is the Father

66) John Piper, The Pleasures of God, Meditations on God's Delight in Being God, Multnomah Pulishers, Inc., Sisters, OR 2000. Pp. 25-26.

67) Thomas Smail, The Forgotten Father, Wm. B. Eerdmans Publishing Co., Grand Rapids, 1980. p. 21

A New Understanding of Jesus: Jesus is Lord

68) Dr Oliver Blosser gave me this insight

69) Quoted by Vincent Taylor, *The Names of JESUS*, London: Macmillan & Co LTD, 1959. p.8

A New Understanding of Ourselves: We are Servants

70) William Barclay, *Daily Study Bible, Philippians;* Westminster Press, 19, pp11-12.

71) I am departing from limiting my attention to Paul and taking Isaiah 42 as a paradigm for understanding the concept of a servant. My primary focus, however, will be on the writings of the Apostle Paul.

72) Author unknown, from *The Pilgrim's Hymnal, 1904, found in The Covenant Hymnal*, Covenant Press, 1973.

73) Chambers. *My Utmost…* September 25

74) Michael Casey, *Toward God: The Ancient Wisdom of Western Prayer*, Liguori, Mo, Liguori/Triumph, 1996, p. 4

75) Rudolf Schlatter, *The Church in the New Testament Period, London, S.P.C.K., 1961, pp. 16-17*

76) James D.G. Dunn, *Jesus and the Spirit*, Philadelphia, The Westminster Press, 1975, pp. 324-325, emphasis Dunn's.

77) Gregory Collins, *The Glenstal Book of Icons*, Collegeville, MN, The Liturgical Press, 2002, pp. 25-28.

78) Rebecca Laird & Michael J. Christensen, *The Heart of Henri Nouwen,* N.Y.: The Crossroad Publishing Company, 2003, pp. 102-103. (The quote is from *Here and Now*, pp. 23-24)

79) Charles Spurgeon, from a pamphlet *Till He Comes* (Taken from a tape on which it was read)

80) D. P. McNeil, D. A. Morrison, H. J. M. Nouwen, *Compassion: A Reflection on the Christian Life,* Garden City, N.Y., Image Books, Doubleday & Co. Inc., 1983, p.4.

81) ibid. p. 8.

82) ibid. p. 6.

83) ibid. p. 6.

Carl Taylor is available for speaking engagements and personal appearances. For more information contact:

Carl Taylor
C/O Advantage Books
P.O. Box 160847
Altamonte Springs, Florida 32716

To purchase additional copies of this book or other books published by Advantage Books call our toll free order number at:
1-888-383-3110 (Book Orders Only)

or visit our bookstore website at:
www.advbookstore.com

Longwood, Florida, USA
"we bring dreams to life"™
www.advbooks.com